Tuscany's Noble Treasures

*Conceptualizing Female Religious
Life in Medieval Italy*

— PAULA CLIFFORD —

Sacristy
Press

Sacristy Press
PO Box 612, Durham, DH1 9HT

www.sacristy.co.uk

First published in 2021 by Sacristy Press, Durham

Sacristy Limited, registered in England & Wales, number 7565667

British Library Cataloguing-in-Publication Data
A catalogue record for the book is available from the British Library

ISBN 978-1-78959-201-6

Contents

General introduction

> ... a very striking feature of this outpouring of grace in times
> such as ours, is the fact that it is conferred in special measure on
> women, "the weaker sex".
>
> Raymond of Capua, The Life of Catherine of Siena *(1395)*[1]

Raymond of Capua's biography of Catherine of Siena, completed in 1395, took him ten years to write, and arguably it marked the end of an era. By then, a period of little more than 150 years had seen the emergence of some remarkable women in the very limited geographical area represented mainly by modern-day Tuscany. Among them, only Catherine continues to enjoy an international reputation. Also well known within the Roman Catholic Church in Europe, but less so outside it, is the recently canonized Angela of Foligno. The rest, who were active in the thirteenth and fourteenth centuries, remain venerated only in and around their hometowns.

Although the holy women discussed in this book seem never to have met, they have much in common. They could all be classed as "mystics": they had intense religious experiences, often in the form of ecstatic visions; their way of life included extreme forms of self-denial; and despite being marked by a "special measure" of grace, they also frequently aroused the hostility of the Catholic Church, which at times felt itself to be under threat from these religious extremists who had seemingly appeared out of nowhere.

Of course, nothing comes out of nowhere, and there are a number of factors that contributed to the conditions which encouraged both new religious movements and individual expressions of religious devotion in the Middle Ages. In general terms, the thirteenth and fourteenth

---

[1] Raymond of Capua, *The Life of Catherine of Siena, First Prologue*, tr. Conleth Kearns (Dublin: Dominicana Publications, 1980 and 1994), p. 3.

centuries in Italy were for many a time of economic prosperity and cultural flourishing, but this had come at the cost of ever-increasing economic disparity between rich and poor. Among the religious Orders, the so-called poverty movements (Spiritual Franciscans, Waldensians, Beguines and Umiliati) were a reaction to both this wider social context and to what they saw as unacceptable wealth within the Church, together with the failure of monastic communities to live up to their founding ideals, notably that of poverty. Alongside this, the enduring popularity of tales of saints from a much earlier time, particularly in northern Italy, and an ever-growing interest in mystical experience all help set the stage for the emergence of new forms of spirituality, manifested by women in particular.

A key source of our knowledge about the Tuscan holy women, and indeed about very many saints of the Middle Ages in Europe, is the medieval enthusiasm for biography. So-called *vitae* (lives), often written in a lively and accessible style, were widely circulated, whether for entertainment (the lives of the Provençal troubadours, for example) or, in the case of the saintly ones, for general edification. Some were constructed with a more specific purpose: to help make a case for canonization. Lives of contemporary saints were sometimes dictated by the subjects themselves, who would then leave their scribes to re-order their thoughts and re-arrange their chronology. It is a rare scribe who can resist the temptation to insert his (rarely her) own views, with the result that the subject of the biography can only be seen through layers of interpretative comment or vested interests, which are generally rather more complex than Raymond's simple view of women as the "weaker sex".

Raymond of Capua, himself a Dominican, was anxious not only to promote his Order's most notable holy woman but also the Order itself, which inevitably influences the way in which he selects and presents key episodes in Catherine's life, much as he had done in his earlier biography of Agnes of Montepulciano. Margaret of Cortona's biographer, Fra Giunta, had done the same for their Franciscan Order. Consequently, the great saints, Dominic and Francis, have their own parts to play in the stories of the holy women, appearing in their dreams and visions, and referenced in the form of worthy monks or magnificent churches, a trait which some later artists would also incorporate into their work.

Another key player in these stories is the Church itself, which enjoyed an often ambiguous relationship with the women whose contemporaries perceived their holiness and whose local followers treated them as saints, heedless of any canonization requirement. Yet these women were on the periphery. And when others sought to follow their example of holy living, the Church had no means of accommodating them, while at the same time trying desperately to restrict the number of new, potentially heretical, Orders that were coming into being. The Dominicans in particular were willing to offer them a physical and spiritual home, and Raymond, in his life of Agnes, was not the only biographer to stress the Catholic orthodoxy of his subject.

It is, however, by virtue of their position in the margins of Church authority that holy women assume a new power. Their mystical experiences, communicated at least in part to their confessors and priests, represent a territory to which few of the latter had access. Furthermore, their often extreme asceticism offered a model of individual community living from which the majority of religious had drifted away, although this would change with a growing movement of clerical and monastic reform. And the growing importance of the laity meant that popular enthusiasm for a local "saint" could not go unremarked.

Yet that power did not go unchecked. The desire of most mystics to receive Holy Communion with increased regularity led to ever more frequent visits to their confessors, and here, of course, male dominance was unquestionable. Some confessors even made contributions to the saints' *vitae*, sometimes with scant regard for confidentiality.

While, in due course, the Church would use the experiences of mystics to help establish such observances as the feasts of the Sacred Heart and of the Five Wounds of Jesus, the local town or city could also turn the presence of a holy woman to their own advantage. Siena is, of course, the prime example, but on a much smaller scale the hill town of Cortona acquired a certain prestige thanks to its own local saint.

In examining the lives and work of these medieval holy women, I am particularly concerned to explore how they are presented and understood by their near contemporaries. What did holiness mean to them, and what means did they use to put that across? The biographies are of key importance; but so too is the interpretation of artists, not least because the social and economic conditions that favoured the development of new forms of religious expression also enabled the emergence of some of the most important artists in pre-Renaissance Italy. Artists and literary writers (most particularly Dante Alighieri), along with those of later centuries, have their own part to play in a developing understanding of "religious" women. Since that understanding was almost wholly developed by men in a markedly patriarchal society, questions of power will never be far away.

The tradition of establishing the reputation of Christian saints for a specific purpose and according to a certain pattern is an ancient one. Think of the portrayal of Peter in Luke's Gospel, and subsequently in Acts. The writer chooses episodes in Peter's life with care, not least his presence at the bedside of Jairus' daughter when Jesus restores her life, foreshadowing Peter's own miraculous restoration of Tabitha (Acts 9:36–41). Even Jesus' prediction that Peter would betray him is accompanied by the promise of redemption ("when once you have turned back, strengthen your brothers": Luke 22:32). Future lives of the saints will similarly highlight temptation, which takes a variety of forms and is usually experienced before they embark fully on the religious life. And when, in the early centuries of Christianity, the stories celebrating the first saints are extended to cover the lives of holy women, parallels with events in the life of Christ are seamlessly applied to them as well, to the extent that by the Middle Ages there is a well-established pattern of hagiographical biography. When a biographer chooses such a form for his work, he is necessarily making a claim for the sanctity of his subject.

The timescale of this investigation is a precise one, beginning in 1226 and ending with the death of Catherine of Siena in 1380. The year 1226 saw the death of Francis of Assisi, by which time his creative approach to worship and his example of extreme poverty had both become established among his followers and would, in different ways, influence the spirituality of the holy women who were to come. It is also the year of the birth of the first of such women, Umiltà of Faenza. Today Faenza is in the province of Emilia-Romagna. However, since Umiltà spent almost all her adult life in Florence, it seems legitimate to bend the geographical boundaries a little here.

In referring to the saints and their associates, I will use the English forms of their names wherever these are in general use, so Margaret of Cortona rather than Margherita, but Umiltà of Faenza rather than Humility.

PART I

Holy women in context

Introduction to Part I

How did the medieval faithful understand holiness? And what sources did writers and artists have to draw on in order to create their own portrayal of a holy woman or man? To answer these questions, we need to go back to a more distant past, and the inspiration of the stories of persecuted saints in the early centuries of the Christian era. And while the names of the holy ones from Syria are not well known today, the way in which their stories are documented is not without relevance to the form of the accounts of medieval saints. What is most striking, however, is the enduring popularity of legendary saints, in particular Katherine of Alexandria, throughout the Middle Ages and beyond. The story of a beautiful woman, who was highly intelligent and of noble birth, and who was prepared to die for her faith, created a particular model of holiness which was appealing to writers, who would celebrate Catherine of Siena for sharing the ancient saint's name, and to artists, who would depict the two Catherines together, thereby ensuring that people would see them as sharing the same quality of sanctity.

It is also worth considering how the ancient tales reached a much later audience. Traders and crusaders were naturally significant in bringing stories back from distant lands, but the medieval delight in pilgrimage to the holy places also played a part. Those pilgrims included women (among them some who themselves would be regarded as holy) who, much like Chaucer's Canterbury pilgrims, would hear and exchange stories along the way.

This spills over into the context of religious life in medieval Italy. The state of the Church and monastic Orders forms a necessary backdrop to the women mystics, whose lives of poverty and self-denial were a wake-up call to those religious communities that had lost sight of their original calling to poverty and chastity. At the same time, the Dominicans in particular offered a safe haven to women who were regarded with suspicion by the Church.

The turbulent politics of the time, along with striking developments in social and cultural life, all fed into the conceptualization of sainthood. For Catherine of Siena this was reflected in her ultimately unsuccessful attempts to bring peace to a divided Church: this saint spoke the truth to those in power, whether they were popes or warring secular rulers. The emergence of the Tuscan dialect as a literary language meant that not only Catherine but Umiltà of Faenza and Angela of Foligno before her would also be remembered as intellectual saints, whose writings had a wider role in the development of the national tongue.

CHAPTER 1

From legend to reality

A legend is a lie that has been whipped up to explain a universal truth. Places where lies and fantasy pepper the earth are particularly apt for the development of these tales.

Carlos Ruiz Zafón[1]

Our medieval forebears were great storytellers. They had an astonishing talent for remembering and reciting lengthy epic poems as well as passing on shorter, perhaps more appealing, stories and adding their own gloss to the narratives they had received from others. And, I suggest, it is in large part thanks to them that we can bridge some unhelpful gaps in Christian history.

It is a big jump from the holy women of the early Christian centuries in the eastern Mediterranean to those who lived in Tuscany many centuries later, and the link between them is easily obscured by some of the major events in European history. The loss of the unifying force of the Roman Empire in the fifth century and the early split between Eastern and Western Christianity meant that traditions of spirituality quickly grew apart and long-lasting differences were created. On the other hand, the seemingly ceaseless movement of peoples from the fifth century onwards enabled the storytellers' voices to be heard and their narratives to spread over a much wider area, crossing the boundaries between East and West, than might otherwise have been the case.

To leave those earlier times unexplored, however briefly, would be to do a disservice to the saintly women and men of the later Middle Ages.

---

[1]   Carlos Ruiz Zafón, *The Labyrinth of the Spirits*, tr. Lucia Graves (London: Weidenfeld & Nicolson, 2017), p. 154.

In the early tales of holiness from both West and East, we see forerunners of the spiritual giants who were to follow. Significantly too, we can see in the interpretation of such stories the gradual emergence of an ideal of a "religious woman", in other words a desire to create a universal truth born out of a time, if not of "lies and fantasy", then of physical danger and social upheaval—a time when storytelling was a welcome point of stability in an increasingly uncertain world.

Legendary saints

Katherine of Alexandria

It is often said that the most popular saint in medieval Europe was St Katherine of Alexandria. Easily recognizable by the wheel with which she is generally depicted, Katherine is a favourite of pre-Renaissance and later artists across the continent. She is present in countless nativity scenes, appearing alongside other well-known saints and various lesser-known local ones, not least in works originating in northern and central Italy. The story of a beautiful and highly intelligent young woman who became an exemplary Christian martyr was widely told and innumerable babies were named Caterina because of it.

The best known of the Tuscan holy women, St Catherine of Siena, is frequently coupled with her namesake from Alexandria. An example of their association is Ambrogio Bergognone's altarpiece (dating from around 1490) created for a chapel in the imposing Charterhouse at Certosa di Pavia, near Milan. It is a pictorial demonstration of the popular association between the two saints, in particular here the mystical marriage to Christ that they are both said to have experienced. In Bergognone's work, entitled variously *Mystical Marriage of St Catherine of Alexandria* and *Virgin and Child with St Katherine of Alexandria and St Catherine of Siena*,[2] the child is placing a ring on the finger of Katherine of Alexandria, while holding a second ring ready for Catherine of Siena. Both women hold symbols of their lives: Katherine of Alexandria has a martyr's palm, while Catherine of Siena is portrayed with the familiar

---

[2]   Now in the National Gallery in London.

lily that symbolizes her virginity. The folds of their robes hint at a mirror image of the two women; but while Katherine of Alexandria wears the red of a martyr, with her beauty suggested by her long blonde hair, Catherine of Siena wears her Dominican habit, her hair, by contrast, fully covered by her veil.

Where, though, did this linkage, this significant development in medieval hagiography, which both perpetuated an ancient legend from the East and enhanced the already considerable reputation of a holy woman much closer to home, come from? In other words, how did the fourth-century story become so familiar and so influential in the Mediterranean world and beyond? Without the Alexandrian saint, would the star of the Tuscan saint and, crucially, of those women who preceded her, have shone so brightly?

The beginnings of the Katherine legend

The Katherine story is a simple one and has some familiar narrative tropes. In outline, it is the tale of a wealthy, well-educated and beautiful young woman, who is widely praised for her piety and good works. She is grieved to see some Christians following the Roman emperor's edict to worship pagan gods, which brings her into conflict with the emperor. The emperor sets up a disputation between Katherine and fifty learned orators about the nature of God and the truth of Christianity which serves only to convert the empress. Katherine is imprisoned and tortured, but a set of lacerating wheels is destroyed by an angel. Eventually she is beheaded and her body taken to Mount Sinai where miracles occur at her tomb.

The story of Katherine's martyrdom probably dates back to the various persecutions of Christians in the third and early fourth centuries. While its association with Alexandria, the second city of the Roman Empire and the centre of Eastern Christianity, and subsequently with Sinai would have helped to keep the oral tradition alive, nothing is written down until the tenth century, the time when the lives of saints written in Latin or in early forms of the medieval Romance languages started to enjoy widespread popularity. Around the same time, Katherine's story received a considerable boost when her remains were supposedly discovered on Mount Sinai, and her relics and the holy oil generated at her tomb entered into wide circulation.

In order to claim Katherine of Alexandria as a direct influence on the lives of medieval holy women, two obstacles need to be overcome. The first is the question of transmission: how did they come into contact with her story at all? And the second has to do with authenticity. It is now recognized that Katherine is not a real-life heroine but a composite figure. How should medieval fact relate to ancient fiction?

The legend spreads

As is widely acknowledged, there needs to be an association with a particular place if a legend, whether based on fact or fiction, is to survive at all. In the case of Katherine, the association is a prestigious one. Alexandria as a seat of learning was the perfect setting in which the story of an intellectual woman could flourish. And Mount Sinai, where Moses is believed to have received the Ten Commandments, was, of course, already a place of religious pilgrimage. So it is perhaps not surprising that Katherine should find a place in Byzantine Christianity, albeit as a minor saint, with her feast day of 25 November being included in the Greek liturgy of Constantinople,[3] well ahead of any recognition in the Western Church.

However, legends and other good stories do not simply require a base. In the Middle Ages, there had to be a significant movement of people in order for those stories to become more widely known. The so-called "pilgrim routes" theory, for example, was formulated over a century ago to explain the growth and transmission of the French *chansons de geste*—the tales of Charlemagne and his associates that eleventh- and twelfth-century pilgrims would hear when they stopped off at different places along the well-trodden route down through France to Compostela in northern Spain.[4] With the preaching of the First Crusade in 1095,

---

[3]   See C. Walsh, *The Cult of St Katherine of Alexandria in Early Medieval Europe* (Farnham: Ashgate, 2007), p. 23. Walsh refers to a seventh-century Syriac Litany, in which Katherine is included as one of a list of "holy women", with her subsequent inclusion in the Greek liturgy dating from the late eighth or early ninth century.

[4]   Notably by Joseph Bédier in a four-volume work entitled *Les Légendes épiques: recherches sur la formation des chansons de geste* (Paris: H. Champion,

further opportunities for storytelling opened up, now bringing in legends from the East, once Constantinople became a rallying point for the final journey to Jerusalem.

The idea of a common pilgrim route as the repository of a legend and subsequently as the source of a literary text was, however, unsatisfactory, not least because it was intended to rule out the possibility of foreign or outside influence. More recently, medievalists have turned their attention to the likelihood of a more general cultural exchange across a much greater geographical area and over a far longer period. In her 2015 introduction to a collection of 2013 conference papers on interculturalism, Stephanie Hathaway writes this:

> Elements evident in literature, art, religion and architecture reveal that the active transmission of ideas across the political and cultural borders throughout the Mediterranean Rim and beyond played an important and central role in the developing cultures of Christian Europe and the Byzantine and Arab civilizations, and since even before the first century AD, setting in motion a quiet undercurrent of multiculturalism.[5]

Hathaway goes on to argue for a "landscape of mutual influence, reciprocity, and an historical process of cross-fertilization in the Mediterranean and its areas of influence from the Roman Empire to the advent of the Renaissance"[6]—influence which covered movement from East to West as well as in the opposite direction, with Christianity being a "key conduit" for the transmission of ideas throughout Europe.

A similar argument has been advanced with respect to the legendary saints from the Syrian Orient, whose stories were in circulation from the fourth century onwards. In the words of Sebastian Brock, "[s]cholars have come increasingly to see how truly cosmopolitan the Mediterranean

---

1908–13).

[5] S. L. Hathaway and D. W. Kim (eds), *Intercultural Transmission in the Medieval Mediterranean* (London: Bloomsbury Academic, 2015), p. xv.

[6] Ibid., p. xvii.

world was, with far more cultural interaction than we had realized, and of a more nuanced kind".[7]

The story of the saint from Alexandria did not, therefore, need a specific "pilgrim route" to flourish and spread. That purpose was also served by all kinds of other movements, to do with trade, slavery, diplomacy and conflict. Clearly, though, at the time of the crusades a heightened religious fervour would have accelerated the whole process, as pilgrims were both eager to seek encouragement in the sufferings of earlier martyrs and keen to bring home relics and other items as souvenirs of their great adventure.

Katherine's popularity had received a further boost with the circulation of a written *passio*, probably dating from the eleventh century, that fixes the oral tradition in a literary form. As the name suggests, a *passio* was that part of a saint's life, more fully commemorated in a *vita*, which related to her martyrdom. This particular text has a number of details that find an echo in the lives of the Tuscan holy women. For example, while it does not include the mystical marriage episode (a likely medieval addition to the legend reflecting a contemporary interest in mystical experience), some of Katherine's last words in this text are addressed to Christ "her husband"—*amor meus rex et sponsus meus*, a word that frequently appears in Raymond of Capua's biography of Catherine of Siena.

By the twelfth century, the story of St Katherine had become a cult, which spread from the Mediterranean to northern Europe. Christine Walsh, in one of her key studies of Katherine, has suggested a movement from Rome, southern Italy and Sicily (under Norman occupation)[8] to northern France and southern England as well as to Germany.[9] She does not consider other parts of the Italian peninsula, but the great trading ports of Genoa and Venice, as well as the movement of Italian

---

[7]   S. P. Brock and S. Ashbrook Harvey, *Holy Women of the Syrian Orient* (updated edition, Berkeley: University of California Press, 1998), p. xiv.

[8]   Diarmaid MacCulloch describes the Norman kingdom in Sicily as "one of the most productive frontiers of cultural exchange between Byzantines, Muslims and Catholic Christians in the Mediterranean world". *A History of Christianity* (London: Allen Lane, 2009), p. 383.

[9]   N. 3 above.

crusaders across the Balkans en route for Jerusalem, would also have been significant in the dissemination of Christian stories and traditions across Tuscany and adjoining areas.

Truth or fiction?

Despite her widespread popularity, Katherine of Alexandria as legend portrays her is generally regarded as a constructed figure, an "ideal" holy martyr. Whether or not that legend has any basis in a real-life figure in the early fourth century is unknown. Critics have pointed out that her name, from the Greek *katharos* meaning "pure", is, as Sherry L. Reames puts it, "suspiciously apt for a virgin martyr, raising the possibility that her legend (like that of Christopher, 'Christ-bearer') may have originated as an allegory".[10] Her feast day was abolished by the Vatican in 1969.

Yet to the medieval storytellers this was not important. Arguably, the lack of cultural precision played into their hands, as they could more easily adapt an ancient story to fit their own ideals. So, as the legend of Katherine became increasingly embellished, it also contained too much of relevance to contemporary religion and society to discard her. And the popularity of the legend with the good and the great—from the crusaders to the Dukes of Normandy—was not something to be dismissed lightly.

The same is true of another legendary saint, Margaret of Antioch (289–304), who is also linked to a place of considerable significance in Christian history. As with Katherine of Alexandria, her name evoked purity—the whiteness of a marguerite. In the East, however, Margaret was known as Marina, another unlikely name, this time intended to create an association with the sea. Margaret's encounter with a dragon meant that she was always suspect, and her story was declared apocryphal as early as 494 by Pope Gelasius, although the Golden Legend says that the dragon incident was not meant to be taken seriously. Devotion to Margaret was revived in the West thanks to the crusaders, although her feast day, established in 1222, has now also been struck out. But what the Margaret cult suggests is that even where the story and the person are openly recognized as mythical, the legend evolves in much the same way

---

[10]   S. L. Reames, "Katherine of Alexandria: introduction", in *Middle English Legends of Women Saints* (Rochester, NY: University of Rochester, 2003).

as the stories of saints whose reality is not in dispute. Their stories are there to encourage the faithful, with the added advantage that a legend can be refashioned to convey a changing message to a changing society. The popularity of these tales was all down to presentation.[11]

There are, of course, other saints about whom still less is known, not least those venerated in the Syrian tradition.[12] There we find, from the late fourth century, Pelagia of Antioch, a converted prostitute (mentioned by St John Chrysostom), whose story bears comparison with Margaret of Cortona; and St Febronia, apparently martyred earlier, during the reign of Diocletian. In common with some of the other Syrian holy women, Pelagia and Febronia were said to be women of great beauty, which through no fault of their own seems to be a recipe for disaster. Unlike the fourth-century desert fathers, the Syrian holy women are not treated as models of ascetic living. Not that details of self-denial are wholly absent from their stories. Bishop John of Ephesus, writing in the sixth century, describes a virgin named Susan who "took up great ascetic practices and virtuous feats of labor, abstinence and devotion", in order to try and gain acceptance in the convent where she lived, spending her nights standing in a corner.[13] Similarly, St Febronia would eat only every other day, if that, and with only a stool to rest on she would "neglect her body in order to subdue it".[14] But like Susan, Febronia had an ulterior motive: near starvation was a way of trying to destroy her distracting physical beauty.

---

[11] As James T. Palmer comments, "Saints who were more legendary than historical were acceptable as long as they were presented correctly". See James T. Palmer, *Early Medieval Hagiography* (Ashland, OH: Arc Humanities Press, 2018), p. 24.

[12] As will be seen in Chapter 9, these early stories tend to emphasize the importance of associated male characters as much as the holiness of the women in question.

[13] Brock and Harvey, *Holy Women of the Syrian Orient*, p. 135.

[14] Ibid., p. 155.

Stories of Syrian holy women

In his sixth-century *Lives of the Eastern Saints*, John of Ephesus writes:

> Since we learn from the divine Paul who said, "In Christ Jesus there is neither male nor female", it seemed to us that we should introduce the story of those who are by nature females, since mention of them in no way lessens this series of stories about holy men. Furthermore, their course of life was not lower than the exalted path upon which every one of these holy men has journeyed, and even their way of life was great and surpasses telling.[15]

Despite this acknowledgement, tales of these holy women generally also include lavish praise of the men who encounter them.

The conversion of the prostitute Pelagia is brought about through the teaching of Nonnos, Bishop of Antioch, and it is recounted by the bishop's deacon Jacob, in a text probably dating from the fifth century.[16] Jacob describes Nonnos as a "glorious man [who] excelled and was most perfect in his whole way of life" and frequently reminds the reader that he is an eyewitness to events which could be understood as a plea for the sanctity of Nonnos as much as for Pelagia. In his preaching, Nonnos is given "weighty and perfect words" by the Holy Spirit and the occasion of Pelagia's baptism by Nonnos is one that "brought great joy to God and his angels in heaven, and on earth to the entire church and its priests". Pelagia then dresses as a man (some clothes being given to her by Nonnos himself) and spends the rest of her life as a recluse on the Mount of Olives. On a visit to the Holy Land Jacob fails to recognize her, and only on her death is her secret revealed, which hitherto was known to Bishop Nonnos alone.

---

[15] Ibid., p. 124.

[16] Ibid., pp. 41–62.

The story of Anastasia is included in a narrative describing the exploits of an Egyptian monk, the late sixth-century Abba Daniel of Sketis, that was also popular in the wider Syrian tradition. It is recounted by a "disciple" of Daniel who, much like the deacon Jacob, also has an active role to play.[17] These are just two instances of women's holiness receiving authority from male witnesses, at least one of whom is regarded as equally great or greater in piety than the woman at the heart of the story.

These Eastern stories read more like fast-moving Arabian Nights' tales than anything comparable in Western Christianity. The sense of imminent danger is acute, presumably because they are all women who dared to be different, and their sufferings at the hands of their persecutors are described in gruesome detail. A recurrent theme is the danger that a beautiful woman presents both to men and to herself, and several of the holy women are described as hiding themselves away so that they might never have to set eyes on a man, so temptation on all sides would be avoided. Despite some unlikely details, the stories all end in the same way, with the women's holiness being fully recognized and venerated, including by established religious leaders.

So then, if these holy women are meant as examples, does it even matter whether or not they existed, whether or not their lives were as eventful as their biographies suggest? It would appear that venerating a legendary saint has not been seen as posing a risk to the truths of Christianity. The question might well be asked that if a popular saint is a construct, does that cast doubt on the veracity of the whole Christian story? It would seem not. As Matthew Woodcock writes:

> Composition and embellishment of a saint's life drawing upon the common stock of motifs and scenarios not only made up for a paucity of historical "facts" but related the individual saint's life to

---

[17] Ibid., pp. 142–9.

the wider saintly community, thus reinforcing the essential theme
of all hagiography: the wonder of "divine goodness and mercy".[18]

The eleventh-century author of the *Passio Sanctae Katharinae
Alexandriensis* claims that he is writing in order to edify the faithful, even
though the Christian faith is not now imperilled by a pagan emperor:
he presents Katherine's story as an uplifting one of victory over sin and
over physical torments. The lives of the holy women of Tuscany will
reflect different elements of that story. For some, Katherine's refusal to
submit to worldly pressures, her rejection of marriage and her disregard
of her physical beauty will be an important model; for others, particularly
well-educated women, her willingness to challenge male scholars and her
undoubted intellectual ability are key factors; while for virtually all of
them her devotion to scripture, her unswerving faithfulness to her faith
in the face of extreme danger, and her interaction with Christ and the
archangel, will inspire their own lives.

The widespread and very detailed knowledge in medieval society of the
story of St Katherine will also contribute to the creation of a subsequent
model of sainthood by writers and artists alike, one which has already
been begun by Katherine's own storyteller.

The role of pilgrimages and crusades

In a society that allowed little space and leisure time to women . . .
religion was the only adequate space for socialization. Pilgrimage
was a special instrument that perfectly combined devotion and
pleasure.[19]

---

[18] M. Woodcock, "Crossovers and afterlife", in Sarah Salih (ed.), *Companion to
Middle English Hagiography* (Woodbridge: D. S. Brewer, 2006), pp. 141–56,
here at p. 141.

[19] Marta González Vázquez, "Women and pilgrimage in medieval Galicia",
in Carlos Andrés González-Paz (ed.), *Women and Pilgrimage in Medieval
Galicia* (Farnham: Ashgate, 2015), p. 29.

The earliest extant account of a Christian pilgrimage dates from the late fourth century and was almost certainly written by a woman of unknown nationality for her "sisters". The *Peregrinatio Etheriae* (or *Egeriae*) recounts Etheria's travels in Egypt and her journey to Constantinople and to Jerusalem, where she stayed for three years. While this incomplete document has been of great interest to liturgists (it contains detailed descriptions of Christian worship at different times in the calendar) and also to philologists (it is a rare written example of so-called Vulgar Latin[20]), relatively little attention has been paid to its feminine authorship.[21] Yet equally important is this early recognition that women who could afford it actually took part in pilgrimages themselves, their safety to some extent aided by the presence of priests and monks. Indeed Etheria and her company were for part of their journey accompanied by Roman soldiers.

Apart from the expense, there were other obstacles. Rome, one of the two main places of pilgrimage in the early Middle Ages, was seen as a place of temptation and especially unsuitable for women. Jerusalem, on the other hand, particularly after the start of the crusades in 1095, was the destination of choice for both men and women, although the journey was hardly likely to be an easy one. For Europeans, there was a third option closer to home: Santiago de Compostela. After the discovery in Compostela of the supposed bones of St James in 814, the city was renamed and became a place of pilgrimage for men and women alike, many of them treading the ancient path across what is now northern Spain, including St Francis of Assisi in 1214. Among the most illustrious of the fourteenth-century women pilgrims were Elizabeth of Portugal, who journeyed there along the Portuguese way from Lisbon in or around 1325 after the death of her husband Denis, and Bridget of Sweden, who

---

[20] Vulgar Latin, as opposed to the classical language, demonstrates the changing form of the spoken language; in the *Etheria*, for example, there are many instances of a recently evolved definite article, which the classical language lacked, derived from a weakened demonstrative adjective (i.e., "that" becomes "the").

[21] See, however, the introduction to a translation of the text by Anne McGowan and Paul F. Bradshaw, *The Pilgrimage of Egeria* (Collegeville, MN: Liturgical Press, 2018), which reflects more generally on women as "religious travellers".

made the pilgrimage with her husband Ulf in 1341. For both women, this was something of a turning point in their spiritual lives. Elizabeth was now free of her unhappy marriage and able to commit herself to Christian service. As for Bridget, her husband fell ill on the way home and would die a few years later in 1344, having spent his final years in a Cistercian monastery.

For women, any pilgrimage, regardless of its destination, offered multiple opportunities. Most obviously, there was the chance to see for themselves places that were associated with the most holy people and events of their faith. They would bring back their own stories of what they had seen and inspire others to follow their example. This was the experience of Ortolana, soon to become the mother of St Clare of Assisi. Like her husband, the devout Ortolana was from a family of *nobiltà cavelleresca*, so well able to afford the expense of a long pilgrimage. Clare's biographer describes how Ortolana, with others, crossed the sea to see the Holy Land with her own eyes, after which she returned home "full of joy".[22]

For others, however, pilgrimage was also a rare opportunity to get away and to socialize. Religious sentiment would thus be accompanied by something rather different: a feeling of excitement that stemmed from an undertaking that, if not dangerous, was certainly daring. As González Vázquez puts it:

> Women's pilgrimage is always exposed to an ideological confrontation, the acceptance of a pious manifestation and the rejection of an activity that exposed women to temptations and dangers to their virtue and the honour of their families.[23]

Once away from home, some pilgrims, both male and female, did indeed behave badly. For others, though, this new-found freedom was felt not so much with respect to domestic constraints as with regard to the Church. When people of faith (or indeed of no faith) come together to engage

---

[22] Tommaso da Celano, *Vita di Chiara d'Assisi*, ed. Giovanni Casoli (5th edn, Rome: Città Nuova, 2012), p. 15.

[23] González Vázquez, n. 19 above, p. 36.

with holy things, in a very different setting from that which they are used to, this may well result in a peculiarly rarefied atmosphere.[24] So it is no coincidence that it was on pilgrimage that mystics as different as Angela of Foligno in the fourteenth century (travelling a short distance from her home town to Assisi) and the fifteenth-century Margery Kempe (who left East Anglia for Jerusalem) should have experienced their most intense ecstasies.

This is, however, a far cry from Etheria, the fourth-century pilgrim who was most probably a nun. Much of Etheria's account reads like a travel guide, and the emotions she may have felt in holy places are mostly kept at arm's length. At Mount Sinai, however, she tells her readers that God called her to climb the mountain, a formidable undertaking:

> These mountains are ascended with infinite toil, for you cannot go up gently by a spiral track, as we say snail-shell wise, but you climb straight up the whole way, as if up a wall, and you must come straight down each mountain until you reach the very foot of the middle one, which is specially called Sinai. By this way, then, at the bidding of Christ our God, and helped by the prayers of the holy men who accompanied us, we arrived at the fourth hour, at the summit of Sinai, the holy mountain of God ... Thus the toil was great, for I had to go up on foot, the ascent being impossible in the saddle, and yet I did not feel the toil ... because I realized that the desire which I had was being fulfilled at God's bidding.[25]

Etheria goes on to describe the church set at the top of Sinai, noting that its priest was "a hale old man ... and an ascetic as they say here ... one who was worthy to be in that place".[26]

---

[24] McGowan and Bradshaw (n. 21 above, p. 35) refer to this as a state of "temporary liminality", but it goes far beyond the bonds of shared experience that they highlight.

[25] M. L. McClure and C. L. Feltoe (eds and tr.), *The Pilgrimage of Etheria* (London: Society for Promoting Christian Knowledge, 1919), pp. 3–4.

[26] Ibid., p. 4.

Later pilgrims brought home more than stories of holy places and the challenges of getting to them. Like all travellers they were also interested in the people they met along the way, as Etheria's comment about the "ascetic" priest already indicates, and they would bring home their own souvenirs, usually in the form of relics of doubtful authenticity. Above all, though, they returned with spiritual experiences to share, whether their own or those of their fellow pilgrims, whose reactions may have taken a form that they had never before encountered.

In short, pilgrimage fostered a freedom of religious expression that, however short-lived, would fire the imagination of those who saw it or heard about it. From the point of view of religious experience, the journey had become at least as important as its destination.

In due course, pilgrimage would take its place as a more general formative experience in the lives of mystics. Bernard McGinn, following E. Cousins, refers to the "mysticism of the historical event", that is, revelations received in historic places in the biblical narrative.[27] So, for example, Bridget of Sweden, on her Holy Land pilgrimage of 1372, experienced a vision of Christ's suffering on the cross at the Church of the Holy Sepulchre, and a vision of the nativity while visiting Bethlehem. While many Christians had become familiar with the holy places, thanks to the accounts of travellers and the work of artists, the ever-increasing opportunities to visit them, then as now, would lead to potentially life-changing experiences.

Crusades

Although undertaking a pilgrimage was largely a matter of individual choice for those who could afford it, the crusading initiative, begun in 1095 when Pope Urban II preached the First Crusade, was rather different. As Jonathan Riley-Smith has argued, while the pope had intended a military campaign to free Jerusalem from Muslim control, undertaken by heroic knights as an act of devotion and loving service to God and the Church, this very concept of war as a penitential act that

---

[27] B. McGinn, *The Varieties of Vernacular Mysticism 1350–1550* (New York: Crossroad Publishing Co., 2012), p. 195.

was open to anyone attracted vast numbers of unsuitable people.[28] Urged on by their understanding of what the Church was offering them, and encouraged by local preaching, "men and women of all classes" set out for the Holy Land.[29]

It was not long, though, before cost proved to be a deterrent, and the crusaders came to resemble more what the pope had originally had in mind. For present purposes perhaps the most significant details are that women were not excluded from this undertaking, and that the sheer number of people involved meant that most people would have known someone who had been a crusader and would have heard their stories. Additionally, there were the relics that, like pilgrims, crusaders brought home with them as souvenirs, and these quickly became objects of local devotion.[30] As a result of the crusades, Christians learnt of new religious experiences, heard stories of hitherto unknown saints, and would find new destinations much closer to home for pilgrimage.

The crusading enterprise had other effects. The Third Crusade in the 1190s was the first to use sea transport in its journey to the East, which brought significant economic benefits to the Italian ports of Genoa, Venice and Pisa, and new opportunities for people to learn of the crusaders' exploits.

By the thirteenth century, however, the whole focus of the crusades had changed. Instead of seeking to win back the holy places of the East, the forces of Christianity began to look inward, either to combat heresy or to reclaim former Christian areas from Muslim occupation, most notably in the Iberian Peninsula and in North Africa. Thus, the Albigensian Crusade (1209–29), the first of a number of crusading undertakings directed against Christians themselves, aimed to remove the Cathar heresy from Provence, and succeeded in wiping out at a stroke the rich

---

[28]   See especially, "The State of Mind of Crusaders to the East", in *The Oxford History of the Crusades*, ed. Jonathan Riley-Smith (Oxford University Press, 1999), pp. 68–89.

[29]   Ibid., p. 68.

[30]   Riley-Smith refers to European churches being "showered" with relics: ibid., p. 75.

culture of Occitania as the whole region was brought under northern control.

As "crusade" came to mean any attack on opponents to papal rule, with both political and religious interests at stake, it could be argued that the conflicts of the thirteenth and fourteenth centuries were not crusades at all. However, particularly with wars directed against the Turks in the fourteenth century, it is worth bearing in mind that these were still undertakings which could involve ordinary people (although less so with the growing presence of the Military Orders), who took advantage of the promise of indulgences. When Catherine of Siena argued for a crusade against the Turks in the 1370s, which was admittedly more in line with the original crusading ideal, her main concern was to support the popes of Rome (Gregory XI and Urban VI) against those of Avignon. Similarly, there is not much of the "crusade" about the military engagements in northern Italy that were designed to make the area safe for the popes to return to Rome. And once the papacy was split by the Great Schism, rival popes at Rome and Avignon did not hesitate to declare "crusades" against each other.[31]

However, the crusades did help to enhance the position of women of a certain social class, who showed themselves to be well capable of administering the affairs of their absent husbands. That, together with the growing cult of the Virgin, would be an important factor in the creation of the figure of an idealized woman, whom the medieval troubadours declared to be the object of their love. The portrayal of holy women in art and literature in the later Middle Ages will owe much to this blending of sacred and secular.

---

[31] Norman Housley comments: "Crusading had . . . turned in on itself in a remarkable and rather unhealthy way, with not only its directing authority, the papacy, but also its chosen instrument, the professional man-at-arms, themselves becoming, in different ways, the object of crusades". See "The Crusading Movement 1274–1700", in Jonathan Riley-Smith (ed.), *The Oxford History of the Crusades*, pp. 258–90, here at p. 269.

Conclusion

The earliest accounts of holy women all help to create an ideal of female saintliness. The storytellers themselves ensure, however, that this ideal is in the "safe" hands of established religion and its male representatives, both by offering the perspective of God-fearing men in the story and by presenting their own comments, as evidenced by the comments of John of Ephesus already quoted. Nonetheless, pilgrims and crusaders of later times did not need to hear this special pleading in order to make the stories of holy women widely known across the Mediterranean world and beyond, helped along, no doubt, by the presence of women in their midst. The accounts of male asceticism, and hints of similar forms of self-denial among women, would also contribute to a more general understanding of holy living.

By the end of the eleventh century, then, the ground was already partly prepared for the outburst of religious expression that characterized the High Middle Ages in central Italy. The process was completed when changes in the Church, along with political and cultural developments, led to the creation of a very particular climate from which a new and rather different group of holy women would emerge.

CHAPTER 2

Contextual realities: The religion and culture of medieval Tuscany

Some follow Law. Some drift (great tomes in hand)
to Medicine, others train in priestly craft.
Some rule by force, as others do by tricks.

Dante, Paradiso (canto 11)[1]

Introduction

The fifth-century collapse of the Roman Empire in the West and the waves of invaders who laid claim to its territories was the start of a period about which much still remains unknown. Undeniably the centuries between, roughly, the fifth century and 1000 AD, once known as the Dark Ages, saw unprecedented social change, in the face of numerous conflicts and vast movements of peoples across Europe. Christianity itself was at times under severe threat, but also at other times was a serious force to be reckoned with. In the West, the Arab occupation of the Iberian Peninsula saw heroic acts of resistance, while the coronation in 800 of the Frankish king Charles the Great as Roman Emperor served to promote the faith across the new Holy Roman Empire.

Throughout the early medieval period, the traditions of asceticism and pilgrimage had a key part to play in the preservation of the cults of saints and in the creation of new ones. Interest in the holy places remained undimmed, while the relics that pilgrims retrieved formed for

---

[1] Dante Alighieri, *The Divine Comedy*, tr. Robin Kirkpatrick (London: Penguin Books, 2012), p. 369.

the faithful a crucial link between the living and the departed, a coming together of earth and heaven. The appetite for an ascetic life, following the early examples of the Desert Fathers of fourth- and fifth-century Egypt, and the Syrian saints a little later, would find a natural home in the development and growth of Western monasticism.

These centuries saw a spectacular growth in the power of the clergy. While the loss of the Roman cultural ethos led to a rapid decline in literacy in the secular world, the monasteries were places where scripture was copied and studied.

Language had a significant part to play in the rise of a clerical elite. After the break-up of the empire, few people other than the clergy were able to understand classical Latin, a purely literary language which had originally been deliberately modelled on classical Greek. On the other hand, the spoken Latin language, which had long been markedly different from the written form, had begun to evolve in new ways, depending on geographical area, influenced by the speech habits of local populations before Latin had been forced upon them. By the ninth century, medieval French had become a recognizably different language. And although it would be another few centuries before the same could be said of the dialects of Italy, Margaret of Cortona in the thirteenth century would still need her confessor and scribe, not just to write down her *Legenda* but also to translate it from her native Italian dialect into Latin. Language, quite simply, was power.

Bernard McGinn has written of the importance of the monastic life in offering a model of order to a wildly disordered world. Beginning with the sixth-century Rule of St Benedict, compiled for monastic communities in the south of Italy, Christians both inside and outside the monastery walls had available to them a rule of life which provided essential stability for anyone who struggled with a desire to escape the world and at the same time an impulse to transform it. McGinn argues that the spirituality of the early Middle Ages was characterized by "an all-pervasive and concrete sense of sacrality based upon clerical dominance and a monastic ethos".[2] People may have been personally inspired by the tales of real or imaginary saints, they may have taken long journeys to venerate holy relics, but at

---

the end of the day they were dependent solely on the clerical hierarchy to teach them the fundamentals of faith, to pardon their sins and to lay down how they should live. In small rural communities, any deviation from this normality would become a source of gossip and scandal locally and, on a wider level, a matter for rebuke and condemnation, as the holy women of central Italy, among many others, would experience for themselves.

Despite the development of an intellectual and powerful elite, Christianity in the early Middle Ages was strongly characterized by more popular forms of religious sentiment. As is still the case today, much of popular religion has to do with death and burial grounds. Peter Brown argues that the cult of saints (or local heroes) centred on cemeteries led to the growth of new Christian settlements outside established towns and cities. These new urban communities "included two unaccustomed and potentially disruptive categories, the women and the poor", who would gather for processions to shrines, local celebrations and so on, and it was in these cemetery areas that women in particular found a certain freedom from male scrutiny.[3] The intellectual giants of the time, Ambrose, Augustine and Jerome, were not impressed and condemned the superstitious overtones attached to the cult of martyrs, which Jerome attributed to the "simplicity of laymen, and certainly, of religious women".[4]

These two disparate strands in Christian society—the elite intellectual monks and clerics on the one hand, and the uneducated faithful with their popular, quasi superstitious beliefs on the other—are encapsulated in the attitudes to pilgrimages and relics. Those who could afford it, women included, travelled to the holy places and worshipped at the new churches that were being built on the real or supposed sites of events at the heart of the Christian story and at the shrines of the great saints. For the majority of Christians, though, their observances took place locally and focused particularly on the relics that the travellers had brought home with them, along with honouring their own local saints. Popular local celebrations and the new religious experiences on offer there were

---

[3]   Peter Brown, *The Cult of the Saints* (Chicago: University of Chicago Press and London: SCM Press, 1981), p. 41.

[4]   Jerome, *Contra Vigilantium* 7, quoted in ibid., p. 28.

particularly significant for women with more restricted lives and narrow horizons. Brown comments: "The saints, as Ambrose pointed out, were the only in-laws that a woman was free to choose."[5]

These contrasting situations and attitudes came to be expressed more generally in terms of two apparently contradictory features of Christianity in the thirteenth and fourteenth centuries: on the one hand the centralization of ecclesiastical power and matters of faith (illustrated particularly clearly in the decrees of the Fourth Lateran Council of 1215); and on the other, the rise of popular religiosity among the laity. The former can be seen as restricting the power of the laity and women in particular, while the latter offered women new opportunities, albeit risky ones.

In summarizing these developments, Professor Chris Wickham suggests that what is new in the later Middle Ages is an "increase in ambiguities":

> Patrilinearity excluded women from inheritance, but gave them more authority as widow-mothers. University education and the professionalism of knowledge excluded women, but a steady widening of lay literacy gave more of them access to books ... *The sharpening of the hierarchy of the church gave more power to celibate men, but lay piety gave a new, even if restricted, space to female religious sensibility.*[6]

---

[5]   N. 3 above, p. 44.

[6]   Chris Wickham, *Medieval Europe* (New Haven: Yale University Press, 2016), p. 194 (emphasis added).

The Fourth Lateran Council

Lateran IV, held in the church of St John Lateran in Rome in 1215, is one of the most important medieval councils of the Church. Much of what its seventy canons contained[7] were reminders rather than innovations,[8] but their effect was widely felt, and several have particular relevance for the development of Tuscan mysticism.

The Council is best known for its exposition, in Canon 1, of the "faith and dogma of transubstantiation". With the growing practice of elevating the Host at the Eucharist, it was an important instruction to the faithful as to what they were actually witnessing, and the doctrine was a key part of the ever-increasing devotion to the Sacrament on the part of holy women and many others. Diarmaid MacCulloch goes so far as to speculate that "celibate women [were] attracted to the thought that the Eucharist gave them real bodily contact with their Saviour",[9] and the language of the holy women we shall be considering certainly seems to bear this out.

Then, most importantly for the development of Tuscan spirituality, there is Canon 21, *omnis utriusque sexus* ("everyone who has reached the years of discretion"). This is the requirement that people should make their confession to their parish priest at least once a year. What is more significant for present purposes, though, is that confession is necessarily followed by Communion; so this canon in effect gives the green light to the practice of receiving Communion much more frequently than had been the norm, and allows those mystics who longed for the Sacrament on an almost daily basis duly to receive it. And as we shall see, where a woman's confessor is also her scribe (as with Margaret of Cortona and Catherine of Siena), this canon contributes significantly to some already complex relationships.

---

[7] The full text of the canons of this Twelfth Ecumenical Council is available at <http://www.intratext.com/X/ENG0431.htm>, accessed 24 September 2021.

[8] For example, Canon 18 reminded bishops, priests, deacons and sub-deacons that they may not perform surgical operations.

[9] Diarmaid MacCulloch, *A History of Christianity* (London: Allen Lane, 2009), pp. 406–7.

Canon 13 forbids the establishment of new religious Orders, "lest too great diversity bring confusion into the Church". This too is a timely warning: while individual mystics of the period are mostly under the wing of one of the great monastic Orders, the need to accommodate their female followers resulted in the expansion of minor Orders, such as Umiltà da Faenza's foundation which was linked with the Vallombrosani movement in Romagna. Nonetheless, religious Orders continued to proliferate, and this ruling was widely disregarded.

Not unrelated to this is Canon 2, which condemns, among others, the doctrines of Joachim of Fiore. It is true that Joachim's teaching had the greatest effect outside Italy, influencing, for example, the Beguines in France. The best known of them was Marguerite Porete, who in 1310 in Paris would be condemned to death for heresy. But the acute awareness of spiritual developments on the fringes of the Church that is shown already in Lateran IV is telling.

In the story of Tuscany's holy women, the continuing significance of religious Orders and of new movements on the fringe, what MacCulloch memorably calls "the wild underworld" of thirteenth-century religion,[10] should not be overlooked.

Monastic Orders in the thirteenth and fourteenth centuries

The main centres of religious life in medieval Europe were communities specially endowed and set apart for the full, lifelong, and irrevocable practice of the Christian life at a level of excellence judged to be impossible outside such a community.[11]

Sir Richard Southern's assessment of the importance of monastic life in the High Middle Ages is no exaggeration, and three of the leading Orders—the Franciscans, Dominicans and to a lesser extent the

---

[10]   Ibid., p. 410.

[11]   R. W. Southern, *Western Society and the Church in the Middle Ages* (Harmondsworth: Penguin Books Ltd, 1970), p. 214.

Augustinians—had a significant part to play in the lives of women who sought such a way of life for themselves. Membership of an Order would lend a structure and respectability to their activities; but it also constrained them, creating a tension that was never fully resolved unless and until they were able to strike out on their own.

It was in monastic life as well that the thirteenth century saw a conflict of ideas that would have a considerable impact on the holy women and their followers, which was to do with the concept of poverty. The newly formulated rule of St Francis demanded a life of poverty, chastity and obedience from his followers. But what did poverty mean? Committed Christians were dedicated to following the example of Christ in their own lives, but was Jesus really poor to the extent of destitution? The Gospels suggest not. On the other hand, his followers were sent out on mission with nothing: "no bread, no bag, no money in their belts" (Mark 6:8), so that they were dependent on the charity of others to survive. Yet even this suggests that they had possessions, even an income, that for this venture they left behind. For the former rich boy Francis, however, poverty meant poverty: in following an apostolic way of living, Franciscans were to have nothing at all; they were to have no means of supporting themselves.

Absolute poverty was attractive to those mystics who followed a path of extreme self-denial. The story of Margaret of Cortona, who became a Franciscan tertiary, shows her even rejecting what little she was given, preferring to hand her food over to the local poor. For her and others like her, the religious life was one of ever more extreme poverty, reminiscent of the ascetic practices of their Syrian predecessors.

For followers of St Dominic, whose Order was given papal authority by Honorius III in 1217 (despite the ruling of Lateran IV), the apostolic life was first and foremost a calling to go out into the world and preach. Poverty, while still necessary, was not to be pursued to the absolute limit—a helpful guide for holy women in Italy and southern France, where the Order became the main protector of women called to community living.

It appears from her biography that the young Catherine of Siena recognized that these different Orders presented her with a dilemma, although she had long made up her mind where her future lay:

> She had a dream in which she saw the Fathers and Founders of the
> various religious orders, amongst them Saint Dominic . . . One
> by one they counselled her to choose this or that religious order
> in which to spend herself in a life of service for the Lord which
> would be more pleasing still in his eyes, and more meritorious
> for herself.[12]

Around 1463, Giovanni di Paolo depicted the scene in Catherine's dream.[13] While the young Catherine, dressed all in white, kneels before an altar, three saints, Francis, Benedict and Dominic, in the darker heavens above, are holding out their habits to her. The artist paints Catherine turned towards Dominic who hands her a lily, symbolizing chastity, along with the black habit of the Dominican. For Catherine, though, her life as a Dominican did not prevent her from emulating the poverty of a Franciscan, and other artists have portrayed her alongside Francis, receiving stigmata as he had done, suggesting perhaps that in the eyes of the artists, at least, the great ones cannot be contained within a single Order.

St Francis and St Clare

It might seem to be a given that St Francis of Assisi should be the most influential figure for all those in that region who followed him in the religious life. The medieval historian George Holmes reflects this in his assessment of Francis:

> [T]he particular form his life took had a special appropriateness
> to the local conditions of Italian society. He was a teacher who

---

[12]   Raymond of Capua, *The Life of Catherine of Siena* (Dublin: Dominicana Publications, 1980), p. 50.

[13]   In panels that were part of the predella of a large altarpiece, forming a narrative cycle that was based on Raymond's biography and was probably commissioned after Catherine's canonization. Three panels are now in the Metropolitan Museum of New York (from the Stoclet Collection).

> embraced complete poverty but expressed a delighted love of
> the physical world, a man of superhuman power who attracted
> simple brothers to establish a new way of life which would excite
> the enthusiasm of ordinary people in a strife-torn society lacking
> religious or political authority ... He provided a model which
> was absolute in both its total orthodoxy and its total radicalism,
> and provoked a constant imitation which gave a distinct colour
> to Italian religious life.[14]

The back story of Francis, the son of a prosperous merchant of Assisi, who renounced his worldly ways for an austere life of poverty, is well known. Admittedly, by the end of the Middle Ages the ideal of poverty, which Francis saw as epitomizing a life lived in imitation of that of Christ, was to fall into disfavour. As Huizinga notes, by the end of the fifteenth century people were beginning to regard poverty as more of a social evil than an apostolic virtue,[15] and there was a growing contrast between the rule of poverty followed by the mendicant Orders and the way of life of people who were truly poor and disadvantaged. Nonetheless, the legacy of both Francis (1182–1226) and his most famous follower, Clare (1193–1253), is of considerable significance for the women who would come after them.

Clare was the daughter of a powerful nobleman in Assisi and, as we shall see, there were many elements in her life which would be echoed, consciously or unconsciously, by the holy women who came after her. At the age of eighteen, Clare ran away from home to join Francis, by then an itinerant preacher, which immediately posed the problem of what to do with the young woman, given that there was nothing to guarantee that other like-minded women would follow her, no guarantee that her perceived vocation was anything other than an embarrassing one-off. Francis' immediate solution was to place her temporarily in the care of Benedictine nuns at San Paolo delle Ancelle di Dio, in Bastia.

---

[14] George Holmes, *Florence, Rome and the Origins of the Renaissance* (Oxford: Oxford University Press, 1986 and 1998), p. 45.

[15] J. Huizinga, *The Waning of the Middle Ages* (1924) (Harmondsworth: Penguin, 1968), p. 174.

But Clare, who was soon to be joined by her sister Catherine (subsequently known as Agnes), was more radical than her new companions. Like Francis, she was not attracted to a form of religious life which retained certain privileges and property, and instead she adopted a rule for a new Order, drawn up for her by Francis, which would come to be known as the Poor Clares. In 1215, Innocent III granted her the "privilege of poverty", which allowed her and her nuns to live entirely on alms. Within a few years there were four houses of Poor Clares, following a way of life harder than that of any other nuns. For forty years, Clare led her community, often suffering serious ill-health, and its numerical growth was proof of the considerable demand for female houses in the thirteenth century. Her rule, the first to be written for women, reflects her own high ideals. Commenting on her steadfastness, Michael Robson writes: "While Francis was a highly acclaimed itinerant preacher, Clare's life of evangelical poverty, contemplation and asceticism reflects more accurately his own thirst for fuller communion with his Creator and his fellow creatures."[16]

Thus Clare sets the pattern for what would become an increasingly familiar story: of women, young and not so young, whose vocation leads them to abandon the life of an ardent lay Christian and to seek spiritual independence in new female communities, where their observances would often be much more demanding than those of their male counterparts. Clare's story is told by Tommaso da Celano (1190–1260), prior to her canonization in 1255. And that story will also set a pattern for biographers of later saints, who seek to impose their own order on the lives of these apparently disordered women.

---

[16]   Michael Robson, *St Francis of Assisi: The Legend and the Life* (London: Geoffrey Chapman, 1997), p. 187.

The Franciscan Spirituals

Despite the obvious attraction felt by lay Christians for the Franciscan Order and its charismatic leader (who was canonized in 1322), its breakaway movement, the Franciscan Spirituals, also commands attention.

The Spirituals, who first emerged in opposition to the mainstream Franciscan movement in the 1240s, were characterized by two things: first, their acceptance of the ideas of Joachim of Fiore (d. 1202) and second, their insistence on the absolute poverty of Christ. Joachim, whose teaching, as mentioned above, had already been condemned by Lateran IV, had divided history into three stages, the second of which, the coming of Antichrist, he believed to be imminent. It was, however, Joachim's third stage that rang alarm bells. This was the age of the "perfectly contemplative church", initiated by "spiritual men". In Bernard McGinn's view, "Joachim's predictions were ready-made for those Franciscans who saw their Order as the culminating form of religious life which was destined to play a decisive role in the imminent crisis of the age."[17]

By the end of the thirteenth century, it is probable that the lifestyle of the Franciscans had become little different from that of other Orders.[18] But this claim to superiority, not helped by the fact that Ubertino of Casale, a leading Spiritual of the time, had declared a couple of popes to be Antichrist,[19] along with the encouragement to live in extreme poverty, drove the Church to react. In 1312, Clement V published his Bull *Exivi de paradiso* ("When I went forth from Paradise") that aimed to clarify the Franciscan Rule and settle the poverty question once and for all, by allowing a use of material things that was "moderated by temperance".[20]

At the height of their popularity, the Spirituals were most influential in southern France and central Italy. And although the division of Franciscans into Spirituals and "Community" suggests a hard-line

---

[17]   McGinn, n. 2 above, p. 73.

[18]   See ibid., p. 74.

[19]   In his *Arbor vitae crucifixae Jesu* (Tree of the crucified life of Jesus).

[20]   *Exivi de paradiso* (On the rules of the Friars Minor). Available at <https://www.papalencyclicals.net/>, accessed 24 September 2021.

separation between the two, in reality it is much more likely that the
ideas and teaching of the Spirituals were in general circulation in Tuscany
in the late thirteenth and early fourteenth centuries. So as Franciscan
tertiaries Margaret of Cortona and Angela of Foligno would not have been
immune to the Spirituals' ideas. The ideal of absolute poverty is reflected
in Margaret's gesture of giving her habit to the poor and wrapping herself
only in the rough mat she used to sleep on. While for some this action
may have been reminiscent of St Francis giving his cloak to a beggar, it
also provoked concern, on grounds of hygiene, among her followers,
although a later artwork, a copy of a lost mural, suggests that lack of
decency might also have been a factor in their disapproval.[21] Conversely,
Ubertino himself is said to have been influenced by the women mystics
connected with the Franciscan movement, which is again suggestive of
a free exchange of ideas at the time.

Dissatisfaction in other Orders

The desire for greater asceticism was not peculiar to the Franciscan
Spirituals. The Benedictines saw a similar movement that began in the
north of Italy and subsequently moved across Europe—the Vallombrosans,
who counted Umiltà of Faenza among their number. The Vallombrosans,
however, remained closely aligned to their Benedictine origins and
enjoyed a close relationship with Cluny, and with the Cistercians, who
also practised a stricter form of Benedictinism. Perhaps because of this
the Order flourished during the Middle Ages and survives to the present
day.

Movements that arise out of a conviction that a community is not being
true to its origins are not uncommon (compare, for example, conservative

---

[21] In the early seventeenth century, watercolour copies of a lost cycle of
wall paintings were submitted as evidence in the process for Margaret's
canonization. These paintings are in the Biblioteca Communale e
dell'Academia Etrusca in Cortona and are reproduced in Joanna Cannon
and André Vauchez, *Margherita of Cortona and the Lorenzetti* (Philadelphia:
Pennsylvania State University Press, 1999).

evangelicalism that seeks to be "Bible-based" above all else). And the development of groups engaging in more extreme ascetic practices, whether within or outside the main Order, was certainly helpful for the holy women of the day. The foundation of new religious communities facilitated the emergence of convents (despite the papal interdict on new communities) and offered a natural home for women whose practices were regarded with some suspicion by the Church. So Umiltà founded an Order of Vallombrosan nuns, characterized by extreme ascetic practices, while Margaret of Cortona founded her own convent of Franciscans.

Dissatisfaction with his Augustinian Order in the fourteenth century led the English monk William of Flete to emigrate to Lecceto in Tuscany where he would be associated with Catherine of Siena towards the end of her life. From there, he wrote a damning letter complaining that "religious in modern times seek the world rather than God".[22]

The great religious Orders, therefore, have a significant role in the lives of holy women, partly because of their greater openness to women, but perhaps more tellingly because their own shortcomings created a climate where their members moved around more freely and formed new groupings with like-minded brothers and, indeed, sisters.

Discord in Church and state

Ahi lasso! Or è stagion de doler tanto
Guittone d'Arezzo (c. 1225–c. 94)[23]

It was not just the disagreement between the normally peaceable Franciscans that affected the lives of at least some of the holy women. Some of them were also drawn into actively addressing the divisions

---

[22] Letter of Friar William to the Provincial of the Province of England, in Benedict Hackett, *William Flete, O.S.A., and Catherine of Siena* (Villanova, PA: Augustinian Press, 1992), p. 161.

[23] "Alas! Now is the time of great sorrow." The Tuscan poet was writing after the battle of Montaperti (4 September 1260) in which the Guelf commune of Florence fell to the Sienese and Ghibelline exiles.

within the Church or into conflicts within and between the powerful city states. Generally they tried to be mediators or peacemakers in complex situations, a role that stood in stark contrast to their personal lifestyle and their search for holiness.

Political life: The Guelfs and the Ghibellines

Although these decidedly un-Italian sounding names first appeared in Florence, they have their origin in what is initially a Germanic conflict between the Emperor Frederick II and the popes. The Guelfs were originally the Welfs, dukes of Bavaria in the twelfth and thirteenth centuries, while the Ghibellines get their name from the castle of Waiblingen, home to Frederick's family, the Hohenstaufen dukes of Swabia. Their hostilities spilled over into northern and central Italy when the Emperor tried to assert his authority over Lombardy and Tuscany, whose leaders looked to Pope Alexander III for support in defending their autonomy. But, as Holmes emphasizes, it was never going to stay that simple.[24] Those embroiled in other local disputes aligned themselves with one side or the other, while tensions between the city states themselves resulted in outright war. In 1266, Charles, Count of Anjou, intervened to ensure victory for the Guelfs. Holmes describes the significance of the formation of a Guelf league, involving most of the Tuscan cities, the pope, France and the Angevin king of Naples:

> It facilitated the involvement of Tuscan Guelf merchants in the business of the wealthiest parts of Europe (that is, Northern France and Flanders) and in the lucrative trade with the under-developed kingdom of Naples. It made Tuscan Guelfs the natural banks of the popes. It encouraged Tuscan interest in the writings and arts of France. The Guelf hegemony is thus an indispensable part of the environment which at the end of the thirteenth century became the world of Dante and Giotto.[25]

---

[24] Holmes sets out the details of the conflict and its resolution: n. 14 above, pp. 4–7.

[25] Ibid., p. 7.

While the early holy women were, then, affected by the Guelf-Ghibelline quarrel directly, the later ones benefited from the cultural developments that followed. Both elements will be important in the way in which the women themselves would come to be portrayed.[26]

The beginnings of schism in the Church

The power of the Church that characterizes the Middle Ages in the West had been building up since the formal break between Rome and Constantinople in 1054, when the Patriarch of Constantinople was excommunicated. While this development would prove to be of lasting damage to the unity of the Christian faith, it was of little or no significance as far as the local faithful were concerned. Much more important in Western Church history—and for the life of Catherine of Siena in particular—was a spat between Philip IV of France and Pope Boniface VIII.

From the mid-1290s, the French king had obliged French clergy to pay a tax to help finance his war with England. Boniface VIII objected and denounced the king, with the result that in 1303 Philip had the pope arrested. This eventually led to the papacy removing itself from Rome and, from 1309, settling in Avignon, where a succession of French-speaking pontiffs remained until 1377, when a reluctant Gregory XI, with much prompting from Catherine of Siena, moved back to Rome. For Catherine, this achievement would be short-lived. The Great Schism began just a year later, when Gregory's successor, Urban VI (1378–89), an Italian, was so unpopular that the cardinals replaced him after only four months with Clement VI (1378-94), who promptly returned to Avignon. So began the period of two popes in power simultaneously, while several attempts to end the schism would for a short spell in the fifteenth century result in the election and presence of a third.

---

26   The terms Guelf and Ghibelline lived on into the fourteenth century, but only with reference to purely local disputes. They were revived in the nineteenth century in the movement for Italian unification: the Neo-Guelfs campaigned for the pope to lead a federation of Italian states, while the Neo-Ghibellines saw the pope as a barrier to unification.

Catherine of Siena's role in trying to end the division ahead of the Great Schism was most likely driven by what Wickham calls a sense that Rome was the "proper" place for the popes to be.[27] As this feeling became increasingly strong in the 1370s, it would cause both Bridget of Sweden and Catherine to be thrust into the limelight of public life.

Cultural life

Literature

The giants of Italian literature of the late medieval period, Dante and Petrarch, inherited a vibrant literary tradition from southern France, that of the Occitan (Provençal) troubadour poets. This group, possibly stimulated by the Arabic verse forms circulating in the Iberian Peninsula, flourished especially in the twelfth century, beginning with Guillaume IX, Duke of Aquitaine, who died in 1127, until the Albigensian Crusade and the loss of political independence in 1209 put an end to the separate cultural developments in the area of Languedoc (now known as Occitanie).[28]

Such was the reputation of the troubadours that their imitators in neighbouring countries chose to write in Occitan rather than in their own languages. At the end of the twelfth century, two of the big names of Occitan poetry, Peire Vidal and Rambaut de Vaqueiras, were working in Genoa and Montferrat respectively, which led directly to the emergence of the first Italian troubadours, among them Peire de la Caravana, an Italian-born Guelf poet, and Rambertino Buvalelli from Bologna (c. 1170–1221), who held posts in Milan and Genoa and dedicated his Occitan love poetry to Beatrice d'Este, the daughter of a Guelf leader.

---

[27]   Wickham, *Medieval Europe*, p. 213.

[28]   This is the area south of a line running east from Bordeaux and passing south of Auvergne. The Provençal language declined after the medieval period to the extent of being (mistakenly) regarded as a dialect of French. In the nineteenth century, it was revived in a more modern form, and today its use is strenuously protected. The names "Languedoc" and "Occitan" derive from an early recognition of the separate words for "yes", which in the south was "oc", as opposed to the "oui" or "oïl" of the north.

The Italian poets frequented the courts of the nobility and often held political appointments, among them Lanfranc Cigala (1225–57), who was a judge in Genoa and ambassador to Provence. Like their Occitan predecessors they did not confine themselves to love songs (*cansos*). The troubadour repertoire included poems known as *sirventes* that were essentially arguments on a whole range of topical subjects, including politics and religion, and songs that were purportedly sung by crusaders. So in possibly the earliest Occitan poem by a native Italian, in 1194 or 1195, Caravana issues a call to the cities of Lombardy to take up arms against the German Emperor, while Cigala's work also includes crusade songs.

However, the lasting legacy of the troubadours, wherever they worked, was their exploration of the themes of courtly love, which were developed in northern France by the writers of the great romances based on Arthurian legend.[29] Typically, the poet takes the role of a humble suppliant, declaring his hopeless passion for an aloof, unattainable, aristocratic lady of outstanding beauty, who is almost always married to someone else. It is a movement that puts women on a pedestal, and its creation of a feminine ideal is helped along by contemporary devotion to the Virgin Mary.[30] Particularly important in all this is the virtue of *mesura*—moderation or discretion—on the part of both the lady and her suitor.

It is worth bearing in mind that there is little linguistic difference between expressions of love for Jesus or his mother and love for one's earthly beloved, either in late Latin or in the emerging vernacular languages. Consequently, the language of a mystic expressing her love for her Saviour in terms of physical human love can appear shockingly

---

[29] Courtly love was first given that name by C. S. Lewis in *The Allegory of Love* (1936).

[30] For a detailed consideration of the cult of the Virgin and its importance in the development in courtly literature, see the landmark study by Marina Warner, *Alone of All Her Sex: The Myth and the Cult of the Virgin Mary* (1976) (Oxford: Oxford University Press, new edition 2016), especially pp. 136–50.

intimate to a modern reader who is accustomed to seeing the two spheres as completely separate.[31]

Dante's devotion to Beatrice and, later, Petrarch's to Laura are in Italy the literary culmination of such ideas.[32] Dante Alighieri (1265–1321), the great Florentine poet best remembered for his *Commedia Divina* (Divine Comedy), takes up the courtly love convention in his early work *Vita Nuova*, composed in the early 1290s. Comprising both poetry and prose, this work already represents a significant departure from the increasingly stereotyped troubadour lyrics, in that it contains an important spiritual dimension. With the death of the unreachable Beatrice at the heart of the work, Dante's expressions of grief are closer to ancient Christian hymns than to secular love poems: her death is an "ascension", her soul once separated from her "enchanting form" is "tender" and "filled with grace".[33]

In the three volumes of the *Divine Comedy*, the poet is guided through Hell and Purgatory by the poet Virgil, and then through Paradise by his beloved Beatrice. Bernard McGinn discusses whether Dante might himself be classed as a mystic, concluding that "The *Commedia* is meant to give the reader hope of seeing God in heaven and also in part in this life",[34] and, as Dante the pilgrim reaches union with God at the end of *Paradiso*, McGinn concludes that there is "no inherent opposition between the vocation of the poet and that of the mystic".[35]

Thus, the circulation of the ideas of courtly love, their dramatization in poetry and the novel, and the almost seamless interaction of expressions of secular and sacred, make a significant contribution to how holy women throughout this period would be presented. Just as secular poetry uses

---

[31] Some worship songs of the late twentieth century, however, reverted to an uncomfortable eroticism, derived from secular pop music, in the expression of a Christian's love for Jesus.

[32] Francesco Petrarca (1304–74) draws heavily on troubadour expression in his sonnets reflecting his unrequited love for an unattainable married woman. Like Dante, he also has something of the Christian mystic about him.

[33] *Vita Nuova*, tr. Mark Musa (Oxford: Oxford University Press, 1992), p. 64.

[34] Bernard McGinn, *The Varieties of Vernacular Mysticism 1350–1550* (New York: Crossroad Publishing Co., 2012), p. 180.

[35] Ibid., p. 192.

the language of the sacred, so the love that the holy women reportedly expressed for their Saviour evokes the language of secular literature. Yet at the same time, they turned the courtly tradition on its head. They now were the suppliants, often using words and images that were much less restrained than those of most, but not all, of the troubadours; while their Jesus, sometimes remote and aloof, sometimes gracious, loving and forgiving, becomes an idealized figure, as indeed does his own mother.

Art

While the holy women themselves would often express themselves in distinctly secular terms, the artists took a different line, depicting female saints alongside the Virgin and often looking much like her as well.

Developments in visual art towards the end of the medieval period were also crucial in popularizing the stories of Tuscany's holy women. Most generally, the prosperous times enjoyed by the city states between the thirteenth and fifteenth centuries resulted in valuable patronage for local artists and enabled new ideas and techniques to flourish. This is the period that produced such great names as the sculptor Niccolò Pisano and his son Giovanni who both worked in Pisa and Florence in the second half of the thirteenth century; the painter Giotto (1267–1337), working in Florence and Assisi in the opening decade of the fourteenth century; and in the fifteenth century Fra Angelico in Florence and Giovanni di Paulo in Siena, all of whom represent the distinctive character of Tuscan art of the time.

George Holmes has pointed out that already in the mid-thirteenth century the art of Tuscany and Umbria was following a different course from trends in the rest of the peninsula.[36] The theme of ancient Rome, so prevalent elsewhere, had little place among people who preferred to use their pictures for devotional purposes. Their painters were, as Holmes puts it, "rooted in local life in a way which made the demands of popular religion dominant",[37] a religion that was above all focused on the central events of Christianity (the birth, death and resurrection of Christ) and the local saints. It is true that by the end of the fifteenth century the influence of Roman paintings had reached Pisa and Siena, but by then

[36]   Holmes, n. 14 above, pp. 150ff.

[37]   Ibid., p. 150.

artists were beginning to branch out in new directions as they combined religious subjects with a new dramatic realism. People and objects were now of interest for themselves, not merely for the devotional feelings they awakened, and there emerged changing representations of human figures and new perceptions of space. Right through until the later years of the Renaissance, Tuscany in general and Siena in particular went its own way.

George Kaftal appears to suggest that Siena was something of a closed shop:

> Foreign ideas and foreign influences were seldom welcome there, nor were the foreign artists. No other school of painters has maintained the purity of its own characteristics so long and so consistently as the Sienese.[38]

Diana Norman, however, draws attention to the stimulus provided either by other artists visiting the region, or Sienese artists travelling to work and study elsewhere. Nonetheless she too highlights a continuity in Sienese paintings, not least because the subject matter of most of them is religious.[39] As one of the patron saints of Siena, the Virgin Mary is widely represented, as are, in the fifteenth century, the two local saints, St Catherine and St Bernardino, as well as other local holy women and men who were given the status of *beati*, and their claims to holiness were enhanced by the art that portrayed them. Norman concludes that while Sienese painting of the period is characterized by a respect for continuity and tradition in the portrayal of religious subjects, this is combined with a capacity for change and innovation.[40]

As we shall see, in their depiction of Tuscan holy women, whether alone or as part of a broader canvas, these local artists and those associated with them could scarcely have been a more effective medium for telling and transforming the stories they inherited.

---

[38] George Kaftal, *St Catherine in Tuscan Painting* (Oxford: Blackfriars, 1948–9), p. 7.

[39] See Diana Norman, *Painting in Late Medieval and Renaissance Siena (1260–1555)* (New Haven: Yale University Press, 2003), especially pp. 33–39.

[40] Ibid., p. 39.

Holy women in the Tuscan hills: Visionaries, mystics or just plain holy?

Introduction to Part II

"I saw visions of God", said the Old Testament prophet Ezekiel (1:1); Daniel's dreams were "the visions of my head" (Daniel 4:13); and in the New Testament St John the Divine saw "heaven opened" (Revelation 19:11). In biblical and apocryphal literature, visions and visionaries abound. Typically the dreamer or visionary finds himself taken up into a heavenly realm, with an angelic being to act as his teacher and guide, often as a way of delivering a prophetic message for lesser mortals.

In medieval literature, stereotyped visionary experiences form the basis of a whole genre of secular writing. Marie de France, writing in the twelfth century, recounts in verse the story of the *Purgatoire S. Patrice* (St Patrick's Purgatory)—a descent into hell via an entrance off the coast of Northern Ireland; while Dante's fourteenth-century *Divine Comedy* takes the whole concept of visiting hell and heaven and turns it into a monumental work, with possibly its own claim to mystical inspiration[1]—but by then visionary experience had already passed into literary convention.

Just as the reality of legendary saints was seemingly unimportant, so too in the Middle Ages the truth or otherwise of such dramatic visions was largely unquestioned. As Bernard McGinn writes, "Throughout its whole history medieval culture was intensely visionary", with contemporary theology and culture adding their own gloss to the experience.[2] In other words, dreams of heavenly places and people, and even more dramatic ecstatic visions, are not necessarily anything out of the ordinary. While visionary experiences may be expected to be part of the lives of holy women (and men), simply having a vision does not make a person holy. McGinn's suggestion of using the term "visualizations" instead of visions

---

[1]   On whether Dante was himself a mystic, see Chapter 2 above, n. 35.

[2]   Bernard McGinn, *The Flowering of Mysticism: Men and Women in the New Mysticism (1200–1350)* (New York: Crossroad Publishing Co., 1998), p. 27.

is helpful in that it conveys better the way in which visions emerge—as an intense meditation on holy things, leading to new ways of seeing the unseeable.[3] And it is helpful too in that it removes the idea that visions are not the special preserve of an elite group of so-called visionaries.

In an earlier volume, McGinn points out that medieval visionaries experienced contact with saints and angels, even with the Virgin Mary, but not with Christ or God.[4] This is what separates, say, Hildegard of Bingen from the Tuscan holy women, for whom the desire to share the suffering of Jesus in his Passion is an integral part of their devotional life and the focus of much of their contact with him. If, then, a propensity to experiencing visions does not in itself constitute holiness, how else are the medieval mystics to be defined?

Essentially, mysticism is not so much an experience (even a dramatically ecstatic one) as a way of life. Characteristically, mystics live in constant awareness of the presence of God. And in order to do that in an authentic way, every aspect of their lives—whether physical or spiritual—needs to be seen in that light: as creating the conditions in which such an intense relationship may be developed. So, for example, Angela of Foligno roots the whole of her life in "humility of heart", which alone can give meaning to her devotional practices:

> For neither abstinence, severe fasting, outward poverty, shabby clothing, outward show of good works, the performance of miracles—none of these amount to anything without humility of heart. Rather, abstinence will become blessed, austerity and shabby clothes will become blessed, good deeds will become blessed and full of life, when they are solidly founded in humility.[5]

In contrast to these firmly articulated directions to her followers, Angela finds her own ecstatic experience beyond description:

---

[3] Ibid., p. 30.

[4] Bernard McGinn, *The Growth of Mysticism* (1994) (London: SCM Press, 1995), p. 326.

[5] Letter to her followers (1305–6), in Salvatore Aliquò and Sergio Andreoli (eds), *Il Libro* (Rome: Città Nuova, 2009), p. 252.

. . . God was embracing my soul. I truly did feel that this was happening. But now it seems that everything we are trying to say about this experience reduces it to a mere trifle, because what took place is so different from what can be said about it. I myself am very ashamed that I cannot find better words to describe it.[6]

Thus ascetic and devotional practices prepare the way for coming into God's presence and are also an inevitable consequence of living in that presence. The lives of the holy women introduced in the next two chapters will offer a variety of illustrations of such living, along with their own particular forms of ecstatic experience.

---

[6]   Cristina Mazzoni (ed.), *Angela of Foligno: Memorial* (Woodbridge: Boydell and Brewer, 1999), p. 148.

CHAPTER 3

Saints in the words of others

She is allowed a voice only inasmuch as she claims Christ is
speaking to her . . . she is legitimate only as a vessel for God.

Julia Lang, writing of Margery Kempe[1]

For most believers, the reputation of saints rests more in their actions
than in their words. It is the reported activities of the earliest Christian
saints that firmly established some in the Church's "communion of saints"
and created legends out of others. Although many of their adventures may
have been subject to distortion and mythmaking, sheer implausibility
alone, such as Margaret of Antioch's encounter with a dragon, is not
enough to dislodge them from popular acceptance. In other words, the
power of the storyteller is absolute.

The same holds true for the lesser-known saints of medieval times.
When little or nothing is heard of their own voices, their reputations
rest largely on the narratives associated with the places where they lived
and worked—enshrined in the monasteries they built, the miracles
they performed, the deaths they died—all stories which are subject to
selection, ordering and interpretation by later biographers and artists.

Some of the best-known saints have, of course, left much more than
this. The actions of a St Francis or a St Clare are complemented by their
well-preserved teaching given to members of the Franciscan Order or

---

[1] Julia Lang, "Mysticism and hysteria: the histories of Margery Kempe and
Anna O", in R. Evans and L. Johnson (eds), *Feminist Readings in Middle
English Literature: The Wife of Bath and All Her Sect* (Abingdon: Routledge,
1994), pp. 88–111, here at p. 100.

the Poor Clares, not to mention a wealth of prayers and other writings. We know how they thought as well as what they did.

For the most part, though, the holy women of central Italy who preceded Catherine of Siena—herself a prolific writer and teacher—are known to us through their experiences and actions as depicted by others. Only occasionally have memorable sayings stuck in the storyteller's mind, such as Clare of Montefalco's "I carry the cross of my Lord Jesus Christ in my heart", which was startlingly understood to have a literal rather than a figurative meaning. There are just two women whose stories are accompanied by writings of their own—Umiltà of Faenza and Angela of Foligno—and they will be the subject of Chapter 4. First, though, this chapter looks at the portrayals of those other holy women who, thanks to the absence of their own words, often seem to resemble more closely the saints of a more distant past.

The "Second Magdalene": Margaret of Cortona (1247–97)

My lover's death, they tell me, saved my soul,
And I have lived to be a light to men,
And gather sinners to the knees of grace.
           Edith Wharton (1862–1937), "Margaret of Cortona"

The stories surrounding St Margaret of Cortona are the stuff of fairy tale and tragedy as well as of religious legend. As a young girl, poor but beautiful, she suffered at the hands of an apparently wicked stepmother. Fleeing from her home in Laviano (Umbria) to the area around Montepulciano, she found work in the home of a young nobleman who quickly moved from being her employer to her lover. Forbidden by convention to marry, they had a child together, before the nobleman was brutally murdered in a forest some nine years later. The man's dog returned home without him and guided Margaret back to the place where her lover had been roughly buried.[2] So Margaret's all too brief time of earthly happiness came to an end.

Margaret's reaction to her lover's death, at least according to her biographer, was to blame herself, and her beauty, for leading him astray, a sentiment that would characterize her spirituality for the rest of her life. In her desolation, Margaret's first instinct was to return with her son to her father's house in Laviano, where she was cruelly turned away. As she sat weeping "under a fig tree in his garden",[3] Margaret heard a voice telling her to go to Cortona, fifteen miles to the north, and commit herself to the care of the Franciscan Friars there. On arriving at Cortona, she was befriended by two women who offered her and her son a home and eventually introduced her to the Franciscans.

Unlike some other saints, including Umiltà of Faenza (see Chapter 4), there is nothing in Margaret's story to suggest that she was a particularly pious child, and her sudden conversion, later commemorated by a chapel near Pozzuolo on the way to Cortona, is unexpected and unexplained. But from then on, that is from around 1273 or 1274 until her death some thirty-five years later, Margaret's life was marked by increasingly extreme penitential practices, while her desire to serve the poor led her to follow the example of the Spiritual Franciscans in adopting a lifestyle of total poverty herself.

After serving a three-year probationary period, Margaret was admitted to the Franciscan Order of Penitents, which in 1289 would become the Third Order of Franciscans. As a penitent she was able to become part of an established religious community and wear distinctive clothing, while living in the city and observing the Franciscan Rule, much as tertiaries do today.

---

[2]   The motif of a dog that is devoted to its master becoming part of the story of two lovers is notably present in French and German versions of the Tristan legend. In one episode, Tristan is in exile, away from Queen Isolde who is looking after his dog, Husdent. Tristan returns to court in disguise, only for his cover to be almost blown by Husdent, who is beside himself with joy at the sight of him. Margaret of Cortona is frequently depicted with a dog, suggestive, perhaps, of an early life that she could never completely set aside.

[3]   *A Tuscan Penitent* (n. 4 below), *Legenda* 1.2, p. 36.

At this point, Margaret's story, insofar as it can be reconstructed, switches abruptly from the genre of medieval romance to that of spiritual history. And just as her colourful early life would come to be enthusiastically fictionalized by writers down the centuries, so too her spiritual struggles would not escape speculative comment. Yet it is possible to see in Margaret an emerging new model of holiness, and in that context her early life is of key importance, however romanticized it might prove to be. Having previously exchanged her poor and unhappy family home for a life of love and wealth with her unnamed lover, Margaret had much to lose in her move to Cortona. Like St Francis before her, she gave up a comfortable existence for a life of poverty. Unlike Francis she made the same sacrifice on behalf of her young son, whom she destined for the monastic life. These extremes of self-denial and the ecstatic experiences that awaited her created a new pattern that is also recognizable in other holy women who were her near contemporaries.

The details of Margaret's growth in holiness are set out in the *Legend* composed in Latin by her confessor, Fra Giunta Bevegnati, and completed in 1308.[4] This is not a chronological description of Margaret's life; it is more an account of a spiritual journey, which is infiltrated by some biographical detail, not always very subtly introduced. Much of the *Legend* is comprised of conversations in which, typically, Margaret poses questions to Jesus, and receives his often lengthy replies. The work is also very much of its time in that it contains a certain amount of special pleading on behalf of the Franciscans and also in its celebration of Cortona, thereby contributing to the creation of a saint of special significance both for religious and civic life.

During her years as a tertiary, Margaret lived first in a cell close to the convent, while her son was sent to be a novice Friar in Arezzo. Fra Giunta's

---

[4]   The most accessible version of this is contained in Fr Cuthbert, O.S.F.C., *A Tuscan Penitent: The Life and Legend of St Margaret of Cortona*, first published in 1907 and republished in the Franciscan Classics series by Tau Cross Books and Media (2016), although his translation is an abridged version of Bevegnati's work. A full edition of the *Legend*, translated and introduced by Thomas Renna (Franciscan Institute Publications, St Bonaventure University, 2012) has a helpful introduction that is particularly strong on historical detail.

emphasis on her penitential practices obscures the fact that Margaret was extremely active in serving the town's poor. With the help of a local nobleman, she founded a hospital, Santa Maria della Misericordia, which cared for the poor as well as the sick, and created a confraternity to run it. She also seems to have had a certain influence in local life, dispensing advice and arbitrating in disputes, most famously rebuking the Bishop of Arezzo for his hostility towards Cortona. Margaret's advocacy for the rebuilding of the church of San Basilio, which had been damaged in the ongoing war between Cortona and neighbouring Arezzo, led to her being closely associated with that church to the extent that it was there that, somewhat to the dismay of the Franciscans, her body was placed after her death.

Fra Giunta and Margaret's *Legenda*

The intermingling of biographical detail and penitential confession is not easily achieved. At the start of the *Legenda* Margaret's back story is rather clumsily put into the mouth of Christ:

> Margaret was in prayer, when the Lord recalled to her grateful memory the history of her vocation, in which, as is quite clear, He included even the years before her vocation.[5]

So Margaret is enjoined to "remember" both her physical and spiritual travails, for example:

> Remember, *poverella*, how then I led thy soul to an utter contempt of all worldly ornaments, and, little by little, did induce thee, in all gentleness and for love of Me, to withdraw from the society of women of the world.
>
> Remember how My grace enabled thy body, hitherto accustomed to delicacies, to abstain, not only from costly meats, but even from ordinary food. And, strengthened by My grace,

---

5   Fr Cuthbert, *A Tuscan Penitent*, p. 36.

and made more bold, thou didst even macerate thy body by continued fasts and didst cast aside soft garments . . . [6]

While much of Fra Giunta's account is apparently based on Margaret's dictated confessions to him, he is also a witness of some key moments in her spiritual development. One such is her longing to be called "child" by her Lord rather than *poverella* (poor little one). Jesus tells her that she must first make her confession, which she did over eight days, calling to mind the sins of her whole life. After receiving Communion, with a penitential rope round her neck, she hears him call her his child:

> Such was the sweetness of His Voice that at the sound Margaret was rapt out of her self and for very joy thought she must die. And in the sweetness of her joy—a joy given to none but those who belong utterly to Christ—she was that day many times raised in ecstasy, becoming unconscious of earthly things, and motionless . . . [7]

All this was witnessed by Fra Giunta himself and several others, including some ladies who "took hold of her, and shook her, and even pulled her hair".[8]

If joy and sweetness are typically used of Margaret's relationship with her Lord, their absence is also marked, as she repeatedly struggles with the temptations prompted by the "envy" of the Devil who she calls the "Evil One", "deceiver of souls" and "seducer of souls". All too frequently Margaret is plagued by anxiety and self-doubt and seeks constant reassurance that she is indeed loved by Jesus. It is, of course, not impossible that Fra Giunta was asking himself the same questions: was his subject delusional, led astray by the "enemy of souls"? So he reports the response of Jesus to Margaret's question about why great gifts have been given to her, who is "so weak in body" and fearful of being deluded:

---

[6]   Ibid., p. 37.

[7]   Ibid., pp. 46–9.

[8]   Ibid., p. 47.

> My child, Margaret, dost thou not desire Me above all things?
> Wouldst thou not willingly die for Me? Art thou not poor for the
> love of Me? Is not thy life just one continuous desire for Me, and
> Me alone? . . . Wherefore love Me as I love thee . . . [9]

As we shall see in the case of more standardized and stereotyped hagiographies, a struggle with the Devil is a requisite element in a saint's development. Most commonly it comes around the time of conversion or similar radical change, no doubt following the pattern of the temptations of Jesus in the time between his baptism and the beginning of his ministry. In the hands of Fra Giunta, though, the portrayal of the second Magdalene seems to demand that Margaret's awareness of her past sin never really leaves her, which logically would imply that she was unable to fully accept divine forgiveness. The result is that Margaret's spiritual insecurity is used to create the impression that the tempter is never far away from her and that the darkness of sin is deep-rooted in her immediate surroundings.

This is reflected in the language of the *Legenda* which is rich in biblical allusions (see further Chapter 8), although direct biblical quotation is rare. Before becoming a tertiary, Margaret worked as a nurse and midwife for the wealthy ladies of Cortona, which prompts her confessor to describe her "as a lily among thorns, as a light in the midst of darkness, or as gold amidst the dust".[10] On the day after the feast of St Thomas, Jesus tells her that he has put her "as a brilliant light to enlighten those who sit in the darkness of sin . . . as a furnace to give warmth in the winter of the world", so that she may draw people to him and be also an example to sinners.[11]

Flowers, light and also sweet smells are all routinely used in medieval hagiographic writing to denote the purity and holiness of the saints. Fra Giunta observes, "As a violet in the fullness of its perfume was Margaret in her humility."[12] Such metaphors also occur more widely. When Margaret prays, "My Lord, pour down Thy blessing upon all who live in the garden of Thy love", it is to the Friars Minor that she is referring, while Christ

---

[9]   Ibid., p. 59.

[10]   Ibid., p. 41.

[11]   Ibid., p. 45.

[12]   Ibid., p. 75.

calls Margaret "my little plant whom I have planted in the garden of the blessed Francis".[13]

Fra Giunta is a haunting presence in Margaret's *Legend*—a confessor who not only relays the penitent's outpourings but who passes comment on her life and takes advantage of this opportunity to reveal, with some pride, his own place in her story and to promote his Franciscan Order (for more detail, see Chapter 9). He is not averse to introducing his own teaching. For example, Margaret, like other holy women, longed to receive Holy Communion with unusual frequency, particularly on holy days, and she often underwent her most profound religious experiences after doing so. One Christmas Day, Margaret hoped to "receive the Bread of Life", only to be told by Christ that she was to wait until the following day and instead stay with Jesus in the "poverty of the stable". Fra Giunta explains this episode with the words: " . . . the better to teach her that this ineffable Sacrament is not to be received without due preparation and a worthy disposition, that she might with greater humility come to receive the great King and be the more hungry for the heavenly food."[14] It is not impossible that besides being an exhortation to proper preparation, this comment reflects his own unease at the practice of frequent Communion, not least by the mystics.

Margaret in art

A portrait of Margaret by an unknown artist, probably a near contemporary, draws attention in particular to the saint's clothing. While Franciscan tertiaries at the time were permitted to wear a distinctive form of dress, there was nothing laid down as to what that should be. Here, and elsewhere, Margaret wears a characteristic checked cloth, which reflects her desire for something rough and uncomfortable. As already mentioned, Margaret is reputed to have given even this away to someone poor and to have dressed herself only in her sleeping mat, which was widely disapproved of for reasons of health and decency.

The same checked cloth is in evidence in an early seventeenth-century work, *The Ecstasy of St Margaret of Cortona* by Giovanni Lanfranco,

---

[13]   Ibid., p. 67.

[14]   Ibid., p. 48.

commissioned in 1622 for the church of Santa Maria Nuova in Cortona.[15] The saint is supported by two angels and her lover's dog is by her feet, as she sees Christ with his wounded hands stretched out to her. By then, however, other artistic influences were at work. The subject of saints in ecstasy obviously gave much greater scope for the artistic imagination. Particularly influential were paintings of St Francis in ecstasy and receiving the stigmata, by Giotto (c. 1290), Giovanni Bellini (1480s) and in particular Caravaggio (1596), and Lanfranco's Baroque-style work stands very much in this tradition. While there is certainly no claim that Margaret ever received stigmata, the marks of the nails in the hands of Christ may well be evocative of the stigmatization of Francis and, later, of Catherine of Siena.

While artistic endeavour has an important part to play in modelling Margaret's holiness, her reputation is perhaps most firmly established not in art but in architecture. The thirteenth-century basilica of St Francis in Assisi had been the first to honour a recent saint, but the city of Cortona was not slow to follow suit in building its own church, the Basilica di Santa Margherita, where the saint's remains are still preserved. Thus was created a bond between the city and its heroine which, in the words of the French medieval scholar André Vauchez, "remains an echo of that civic and lay religiosity that constituted one of the most original features of the civilization of the Italian commune at its apogee".[16]

The end of Fra Giunta's narrative similarly brings together Margaret the civic leader and Margaret the miracle worker:

> When the people of Cortona heard of the death of Margaret, calling together a council of the citizens, they went to the church of St Basil and there . . . they buried [her body] in a new sepulchre,

---

[15]   Margaret's canonization process ran from 1629 to 1640, and scenes from her life would have been common at this time.

[16]   Joanna Cannon and André Vauchez, *Margherita of Cortona and the Lorenzetti: Sienese Art and the Cult of a Holy Woman in Medieval Tuscany* (Philadelphia: Pennsylvania State University Press, 1999), p. 224.

many clerics and religious being present. And here, according to the promises made her by God, many miracles were wrought.[17]

Twentieth-century inspiration

Unlike her Tuscan contemporaries, the colourful story of Margaret of Cortona has inspired both devotion and literary creativity. As a "civic" saint, she was attributed with keeping Cortona free from the cholera plague that struck in the second half of the nineteenth century, when the church of S. Margherita was rebuilt in gratitude; while in the mid-twentieth century Margaret was honoured for having protected Cortona during World War II, despite the fighting in nearby Arezzo.

In France, Margaret was the inspiration for the Catholic novelist François Mauriac, who wrote what he called "the story of a soul" while living in occupied France.[18] Mauriac's *Margaret of Cortona* is essentially a meditation on Margaret's *Legend*, overlaid with his emotions at the fate of his country: "The martyrdom of the girl from Cortona distracted me from the martyrdom of my country", he claims—a distraction from his overwhelming frustration at his own powerlessness:

> Later I came back to Paris to find shelter and contribute to the clandestine press. But those dark days before the Resistance, in a countryside drenched with rain or wasted with sun, where I suffered a boredom beyond anything I had known at any other moment of my life—these days are incarnated for me in this little mad saint, intent on destroying her beautiful face which, after years of savage penance, still frightened the Friars of Cortona.[19]

Mauriac the novelist does not make things up, but he meditates on what might have been. As he comes to reflect on Margaret's death, his thoughts turn to Margaret's abandoned son:

---

[17]   Fr Cuthbert, *A Tuscan Penitent*, p. 124.

[18]   François Mauriac, *Margaret of Cortona* (1943), tr. Barbara Wall (London: Burns, Oates and Washbourne, 1948), p. 2.

[19]   Ibid., p. 3.

[Fra Giunta] does not tell us whether her unhappy child was at his mother's bedside. It is not a happy fate, at least in this world, to be the son of a saint unless one has become a saint oneself . . . Perhaps he pushed aside the sacrilegious thought: "*She* has had her period of happiness on earth, a full and flaming youth, whereas I . . . ". But perhaps too she had inspired in him a desire to follow her along the unknown road, and perhaps he, a fervent religious, envied his mother for having reached the end of the exhausting earthly journey.[20]

Thoughts of what might have been also permeate Edith Wharton's poem similarly entitled "Margaret of Cortona". When it was published in 1901, it caused a furore in the Roman Catholic Church, with its suggestion that if Margaret had been faced with a choice between her lover somehow escaping his mortal fate and a life dedicated to following Christ, she would have opted for the former. Wharton had herself been disappointed in love and she too imagines Margaret on her deathbed:

> I say: Suppose my lover had not died—
> Think you I ever would have left him living,
> Even to be Christ's blessed Margaret?

Then the poet goes for the jugular:

> He was my Christ—he led me out of hell—
> He died to save me (so your casuists say!)—
> Could Christ do more? Your Christ outpity mine?
> Why *yours* but let the sinner bathe His feet;
> Mine raised her to the level of his heart . . . [21]

---

[20]   Ibid., p. 135.

[21]   Edith Wharton, "Margaret of Cortona", in Louis Auchincloss (ed.), *Edith Wharton: Selected Poems* (Literary Classics of America, 2005), pp. 43–9. The poem is available at <https://internetpoem.com/edith-wharton/margaret-of-cortona-poem/>, accessed 24 September 2021.

It is striking that a saint so little known outside her own region (which for Mauriac was part of her attraction) should speak so directly to the experience of two important literary figures of a later age. While Mauriac, the intense Catholic, is able to reflect on some of the more profound spiritual details in the *Legend*, Wharton, who might have contemplated becoming a Catholic herself, questions their usefulness. Both, however, are inexorably drawn to Margaret's early life, rather than to her redemption, for their inspiration. The same might well have been true of Fra Giunta as well, whose discomfort at his subject's origins never completely died away.

Upholding the truth: Clare of Montefalco (1268–1308)

*"I will not be afraid, because I carry the cross
of my Lord Jesus Christ in my heart."*

A model of orthodoxy

While the majority of holy women discussed here embraced a life of holiness only as adults, Clare of Montefalco, also known as St Clare of the Cross, offers a new model, that we will see repeated in the life of Catherine of Siena, that of holiness since early childhood. Although, in general, childhood was rarely seen as significant in human development until relatively modern times, the faith of saints in their earliest years became part of a fixed hagiographic form in the late Middle Ages (see the section on visionaries below). At a time when heresy was rife, Clare's early life offered an opportunity to emphasize the importance of lifelong faithfulness to the Church and its teaching.

Clare was born into a family that was not only intensely religious (her parents were Third Order Franciscans) but also wealthy. Thanks to the generosity of their father, Damiano Vengente, Clare's older sister Giovanna was able to live as a Franciscan Tertiary in a *reclusorio* (hermitage) that he built for her. At the age of just six, with the full consent of her parents and with the eventual blessing of the Church, Clare became a tertiary like her sister and moved in with her. Her life of obedience, then, began with being subject to Giovanna, named as Superior, who both encouraged Clare in her vocation and rebuked her when her austerity became excessive. Within four years, the sisters had been joined by other young women or children and moved into a larger house again provided by Damiano. After sixteen years as lay penitents, Clare and Giovanna both became Augustinian nuns, with Giovanna named as abbess in her father's house, now dedicated as a convent.

We have no direct record of Clare's spirituality or theology. Her biographer, the French-born Berengario di Sant'Africano, never met her; his task, in his role as vicar to the Archbishop of Spoleta, was to prepare a document for her canonization process which was ordered in the year after her death. It is possible that his account (in Latin) of her life and miracles was completed as early as 1310, although it could well have been a few years later. In 1318, at the third attempt, a process was opened at Montefalco but was unsuccessful. Although Clare wrote nothing herself, her younger brother Francesco, a Friar Minor, gave evidence at the process and it is reasonable to suppose that he could have been the source of at least some of the words attributed to her by Berengario.

Community life is far from solitary, and it is Clare's visions, surely well known to her sisters and reported more widely by them and their associates, that reveal the essence of her spirituality. Berengario reports her many visions in childhood of the Virgin Mary and the child Jesus at the same age as Clare—he plays with her and comforts her, and it seems they enjoy the physical contact that children naturally establish. As Clare grows older, that physicality translates into a devotion to the body of Christ crucified, and the cross becomes the centre of her existence.

This focus on the Passion is characteristic of later medieval spirituality. For Clare, however, it takes a distinctively physical form. She has a vision of Christ walking the world (reminiscent here of the legend of the wandering Jew), looking for somewhere to plant his cross, in response to which Clare offers her heart. She also has a vision of the three nails of the cross—one large, for Christ's feet, two smaller ones for his hands—which she is characteristically depicted by artists as holding. The story goes that after her death her heart was opened up, to reveal these nails in miniature. Similarly her gall bladder contained three gallstones, which would explain why she spent her later years in considerable pain.

Clare's other reported visions include visions of heaven and the saints, of God as judge, and of souls (including her now dead sister Giovanna) in Purgatory.

The Free Spirit heresy

Since the early days of Christianity, people who aspired to come closer to God by extreme forms of self-denial could do so while being part of, or closely associated with, a religious Order and without falling foul of the teaching of the Church. Holy women were no exception: although their choice of ascetic practices may have set them apart from their families or companions, they could remain part of their own communities and were cared for by them. Groups such as the Franciscan Spirituals and the Vallombrosans were outside the mainstream but were nonetheless not condemned as heretics. The so-called Free Spirit heresy, however, was something else. Like members of the main religious Orders, its adherents sought to come close to God, but not through the good offices of the Church.

The heresy of the Free Spirit is at one level a medieval reincarnation of the heresy of antinomianism which dogged Christianity almost from the start.[22] One of the best-known exponents of a refinement of this teaching, Marguerite Porete, was condemned and burnt in Paris in 1310, leaving behind her *Mirror of Simple Souls*.[23] Her argument was that once human beings had

---

[22] Significant parts of the Johannine epistles are clearly directed at believers who hold that since Christians enjoy the promise of forgiveness they can basically behave as they like.

[23] The full title is *Le mirouer des simples âmes anienties et qui seulement demourent en vouloir et desir d'amour* (*The mirror of simple annihilated souls and those who only remain in will and desire of love*). English editions include that by Ellen Babinsky in the Classics of Western Spirituality series (New York: Paulist Press, 1993), and there is a modern French version published by Albin Michel (1984, 2021). The "*âmes anienties*" refers to the soul's annihilation in God.

achieved perfection in this life, they were incapable of sin, however they might choose to live.

This search for spiritual perfection was inspired by a desire for oneness with God which, of course, would have been shared by believers within the Church. Some of the best-known mystics in different parts of Europe set out their own ideas on the "steps" by which believers might achieve perfection.

The Free Spirit movement—its first female followers were known as Beguines—was a movement that may have been born out of fear of events that many in the thirteenth century saw as presaging apocalypse: wars, plague and so on. More significantly, however, it was a lay movement, comprised more of individuals than of groups, that rejected the authority of the clergy and the need for the sacraments. After Marguerite's death, the Council of Vienne (1311–12) detailed eight objections to the Beguines' teaching,[24] and cited Germany, in particular, where there were also male adherents (Beghards). As a consequence of the doctrine of impeccability—"a degree of perfection which renders [a person] utterly impeccable and unable to make further progress in grace"—the Beguines had no need to fast or pray, nor to be subject to any form of human obedience, including "the commandments of the Church". And an obvious source of scandal was their belief that kissing was a mortal sin "since nature does not incline one to it" but the act of intercourse was not, since it was "an inclination of nature".

The Council's conclusion was to "condemn and utterly reject" the movement and to encourage the Church's "diocesans and inquisitors of heresy for the regions where these Beghards and Beguines live" to make careful inquiries about their beliefs and behaviours, and to impose due punishment on the guilty ones, "unless there is voluntary abjuration of [their] errors and repentance with fitting satisfaction".

---

24   The documents of the Council are available at <https://www.papalencyclicals. net/councils/ecum15.htm>, accessed 24 September 2021.

Clare's condemnation

Clare is often credited with confronting the Free Spirit heresy and with responsibility for removing it from central Italy. This is, however, something of an over-statement. Clare's contact with the heresy amounted to little more than a chance encounter.

The founder of the Italian equivalent of the Free Spirit movement, referred to as the heresy of the *spirito della libertà*, was a Franciscan called Bentivenga da Gubbio. Bentivenga, who was admired for his holy lifestyle, and is known to have been in Montefalco in 1306, when he was *predicatore* (preacher) at the Franciscan monastery, which was closely aligned to Clare's S. Croce convent. But Bentivenga already had history: before becoming a Franciscan, he had been a member of the "Apostoli" sect,[25] suppressed in 1286 by Pope Honorius IV, who ordered its members to join one of the Orders approved by the Church instead. At about this time, according to Berengario's *Vita,* there appeared first in the Duchy of Spoleto and then in Umbria the phenomenon of processions of *flagellanti*—men and women who moved around the countryside in a state of undress, flagellating themselves in displays of penitence.

Berengario's account is the only testimony to one of Clare's visions in which she sees a crowd of *flagellanti* gathered round a crucifix, worshipping its figure in noisy disarray. In her dream, Clare recognizes this as being not of God but of the Devil. When Bentivenga arrived in Montefalco a couple of years later, he tried to win Clare over to his ideas, in conversations reported by Berengario, only to be denounced by her early in 1307. This led to his arrest and his eventual life imprisonment, a sentence which he served out in S. Croce in Florence, where he died in 1332.

Although this episode contributed to the removal of the Free Spirit heretics from Spoleto, they did not disappear from Italy completely. Berengario's account, written, of course, in the light of Pope Clement V's condemnation of the sect at Vienne, seems to be designed as an illustration of Clare's zeal for the Church. And given her enduring

---

[25]   The *Apostoli*, or Apostolic Brethren, date from the 1260s. Founded in northern Italy they advocated total poverty and sought a life of complete holiness, while preaching an apocalyptic message and, crucially, failing to submit to the authority of the Church.

dedication to living a life of total obedience, it is not hard to see why a heresy that openly advocated disobedience to the Church's teaching should have been particularly abhorrent to her.

There may have been more personal reasons as well. As Klotz has pointed out, some of Clare's practices appeared to be uncomfortably close to those advocated by the heretics:

> ... she was often elevated into union with God through her raptures, prayers and visions ... She had reached glimpses of union with God in this earthly life, which was one of the goals of the sect of the Free Spirit ... her lifestyle was one of self-abnegation and self-denial and there were many times when she was completely unaware of her physical body.[26]

Although this was offset, as Klotz stresses, by Clare's devotion to the sacraments of the Church and by her many contacts within the Church hierarchy, the canonization process needed to be seen to remove any suspicion of closer links with the sect Clare was so keen to root out.

Clare in art

Unsurprisingly, for a saint whose whole being appears to have been centred on the cross of Christ, Clare of Montefalco is most often depicted either in the context of crucifixion, or holding her own heart, which is reputed, when opened up after her death, to have contained in miniature the instruments of crucifixion. The Santuario di S. Chiara della Croce in Montefalco has a fourteenth-century fresco by an unknown Umbrian artist of Christ presenting Clare with a substantial cross that she is pressing into her body—an active movement that belies any suggestion of passive reception.

A notable exception to this theme, however, is a fresco of Clare as a child playing, or trying to play, with the Christ child of comparable age, although his mother seems to be shielding him from close contact with her.

---

[26] Margaret E. Klotz, OSF, *Clare of Montefalco (1268–1308): The Life of the Soul is the Love of God* (Doctoral thesis, Faculty of Theology, University of St Michael's College, Toronto, 2001), p. 161.

Agnes of Montepulciano (1268–1317)

Montepulciano is an ancient hill town about forty miles south-east of Siena, which in the fourteenth century was part of the diocese of Arezzo. Famous for its wine and culture, Montepulciano was a rich target for the rival powers of Florence and Siena throughout the Middle Ages, reverting to Florence in 1390 after more than 150 years of Sienese control.

Agnes Segni was born in the nearby village of Gracciano. Like Clare of Montefalco, she was only nine when she asked to join an Order of Dominican nuns, whose penitential garments caught her attention. Six years later she was among a group of sisters who established a new convent at the town of Proceno on the Via Francigena and where she lived for the next twenty-two years. During this time, her fame grew, since for fifteen years she is said to have lived on bread and water. She deprived herself of sleep and had a passion for the Eucharist, occasionally receiving bread and wine from the hands of angels.

Agnes' eating habits inspired great admiration in Catherine of Siena, who understood that Agnes' provision for her sisters was a matter of faith. So, as with other women saints, her own extreme fasting was accompanied by tales of miraculous feeding of others, in particular the multiplication of bread and oil. Catherine's *Dialogue* describes how, whereas angels had provided food for the young St Dominic and his brothers "without any human intermediary", Agnes' miracle of multiplication fed her and her new community of eighteen young virgins, after God had allowed them to go "three days without bread with nothing but greens to eat".[27] Agnes' calling was to tend, and at times miraculously heal, the sick people around her, rather than deliberately seek engagement with the world. However, she also seems to have had some role in local politics. Returning to Montepulciano after her time in Proceno, she became involved in mediating in disputes between noble families, who, without an outside enemy to fight, resorted to combat with each other. Such was the ferocity of this "great dissension" that the local nobility came to Agnes to beg her

---

[27] *Catherine of Siena: The Dialogue*, tr. Suzanne Noffke, Classics of Western Spirituality (New York: Paulist Press, 1980), pp. 314, 315.

to pray for the land which they felt to be in danger. Agnes duly summoned her sisters to prayer and was herself moved to tears:

> Pray and beseech, daughters, as fervently as you can, because I see clearly many future tribulations for this land. For the Lord permits dissensions to arise on account of their sins among the citizens and especially among the nobles and the rulers, from whom great scandals will come forth and no small war, in such a way that not only will this city become desolate, but the whole of Tuscany will be troubled from this cause.[28]

And indeed, as her biographer notes, the dissensions led to oppressive wars, just as Agnes had predicted.

Given the uncertain state of Tuscany at the time, this fulfilment of prophecy does not come as a great surprise. And there is little otherwise to suggest that Agnes' saintliness and diplomacy was anything more than would have been displayed by any other head of a religious community.

The only other reference to a gift of prophecy in Agnes' *Life* relates to her insight into her sisters' thoughts, knowing "the secret thoughts of hearts",[29] which had the effect of disciplining the women to think only what was good.

After Agnes' death her body exuded what Walker Bynum calls "marvellous effluvia",[30] that is, liquids with healing powers. In the lifetime of medieval holy women this allegedly replaced the natural secretions of menstrual blood and breastmilk, and in the case of Agnes it seems to have fulfilled the function of embalming fluid—her body showed no signs of decay many years later.

---

[28]   Raymond of Capua, *The Life of Saint Agnes of Montepulciano*, tr. Sister Mary Martin Jacobs, OP (Summit, NJ: DNS Publications, 2012), p. 86.

[29]   Ibid., p. 85.

[30]   Caroline Walker Bynum, *Holy Feast and Holy Fast: The Religious Significance of Food to Medieval Women* (Berkeley: University of California Press, 1992), p. 273.

A shared biographer

Agnes owes much of her reputation to her biographer Raymond of Capua, who would later write a much more substantial biography of Catherine of Siena. Although Agnes died thirty years before Catherine was born, her story would have been well known in Siena, and her influence on Catherine would become definitive thanks to Raymond. The joint theme of excessive abstinence and miraculous feeding is clearly a source of fascination, and he appears to have told Catherine everything he knew of Agnes' life. Having visited Agnes' tomb (in 1367) some fifty years after her death and discovered that her body remained virtually intact, Raymond ensured that this became widely known. And when eventually Raymond took Catherine to visit Montepulciano, he stepped well outside the conventional role of a biographer and became an active participant and influencer in the drama of the lives of both women.

In the course of his biography, Raymond is given to special pleading on Agnes' behalf. He freely acknowledges, for example, that it was not unknown for solitaries—those without a human minister—to receive Communion from angels, but, he adds, "to those having an abundance of ministers . . . you will rarely find any". Raymond is quick to argue that this "singular privilege" does not necessarily raise Agnes above other saints: it is simply that "each saint has something particular to himself [*sic*] that is not found in others".[31]

As the story of Agnes' life draws to a close, Raymond becomes ever bolder in his biblical parallels, to the extent of aligning himself with the writer of John's Gospel. Immediately before the account of her death he comments:

> Many other signs Jesus did through the virgin Agnes, his living spouse, which are not written in this book, but these are written that you might believe, and that, believing, you might receive her help before the Lord (John 20:30–31).[32]

---

[31] N. 28 above, p. 31.

[32] Ibid., p. 87.

In the prologue to Part III, which deals with events after the saint's death, Raymond continues in a similar vein, this time referencing the book of Revelation and apparently comparing the book referred to in Revelation 5 with his own:

> "Worthy are you, Lord, to receive this book and open its seals" (Revelation 5:9). If this scripture verse is applied to our subject, we will see that the Lamb, Agnes' Spouse, was worthy to receive, not a mutilated book, but a complete one.

While Agnes has previously been referred to as the Spouse of the Lamb,[33] now there is a direct comparison with the Lamb himself:

> . . . one must manifestly conclude that Agnes, insofar as she was like the Lamb, is worthy to receive from our littleness not an incomplete book, but a perfect and finished one, she herself resolving and making clear all doubtful passages,[34]

although Raymond suggests that it is the Lord himself rather than Agnes who has helped him in completing his task.

Agnes and the cult of relics

Medieval devotion to relics and pilgrimage has a part to play both during Agnes' life and after it. Unsurprisingly, given the preoccupations of the time, Agnes longs to visit the Holy Land, but her prayers that she might do so are answered in a different way. As she prays and weeps, she finds her hand full of earth:

> It was revealed to her by an angel from the Lord that this soil which she had received came from the place where the Savior

---

[33]   Raymond argues at the start of his work that the name Agnes is derived from *agna*, a ewe-lamb or "spouse of a Lamb" (*Life*, pp. 3–4). See further pp. 168–9 below.

[34]   Ibid., p. 93.

of the world, hanging on the cross for our sins, had soaked the ground with his blood.

The angel also brought her, for her greater consolation, a piece of that basin in which our Savior when he was of tender age took a bath in the manner of little children.[35]

These somewhat unusual relics she puts in a safe place along with unspecified other items. It is an episode which seems to be intended to enhance the importance of the cult of relics by depicting them as a direct gift from God to the faithful.

This is echoed in a later event, when Agnes visits the tombs of Peter and Paul in Rome. Overwhelmed by a desire to possess something of theirs, she prays for relics to be given to her, and receives two pieces of clothing, one cut "from the garments of the first Vicar of Jesus Christ and the other from the cloak of the Teacher of the Gentiles",[36] their significance being explained to her by God.

The miracles associated with Agnes after her death also appear to promote the cult of relics already discussed. Part III of Raymond of Capua's *Legenda* is above all a plea to recognize her sanctity, beginning with references to miracles immediately following her death, which were, of course, a necessary requirement for canonization (see further Chapter 10 below). At first, recipients of her miraculous healing came to touch her body, a duty made all the more pleasant and memorable by the aroma emanating from it. Raymond comments: "As she drew the faithful after her in life by a spiritual light, she attracted them also after death by a physical fragrance."[37]

Subsequently, however, as a pilgrim movement of people began to gather pace, some received healing before coming near to the saint:

The sick began to come from remote and far off places to the church of Agnes, and all reported the favour of perfect health.

---

[35] Ibid., p. 33.

[36] Ibid., p. 34.

[37] Ibid., p. 95. Raymond introduces his comment with a reference to Matthew 5:15 and the lamp that could not be hidden under a bushel.

> Some of these, because, I suppose, they had greater faith in
> her sanctity, as soon as they crossed the bridge approaching
> her church but before they entered the church itself, already
> felt themselves to be completely free of their illness. Others,
> however, because, as I assume, they were led by the vehicle of a
> lesser faith, on entering the church itself immediately received
> perfect health.[38]

Almost immediately, though, such healings cease to be confined to the
petitioner's close physical proximity to the saint. A simple promise to
visit is sufficient. So there follows a catalogue of miracles where the saint
responds to prayer with immediate healing once the petitioner has vowed
to visit her relics, often with the addition of more elaborate promises. So,
for example, the account of a man struck by an illness that deprived him
of the use of his legs and tongue:

> After much suffering, despairing of any natural remedy, he
> devoutly promised the holy virgin in his mind, that if by her
> assistance he received back the use of his members, he would
> go to her church naked . . . bringing a wax *ex voto* in her honor.
> Having made this vow mentally, immediately, without any lapse
> of time, he received what he had devoutly requested by the merits
> of the virgin Agnes. Completing by deeds what he had solemnly
> promised in his mind, he narrated the present miracle before a
> notary public and witnesses whom I know well, with an oath.[39]

The need to present a case for canonization with a legally certified claim
is evident here. However, it also reflects the importance of relics and
pilgrimage, and Raymond here adds another local shrine to the ever-
increasing number of destinations. The significance of the shrine is greatly
enhanced by the fact that a condition of the miracles attributed to Agnes
after her death is that the recipient should visit her relics. Raymond's
account of such miracles enumerates them in a way that evokes those

---

[38] Ibid., p. 98.

[39] Ibid., p. 118.

proclaimed in prophecies of the Messiah or seen in the actions of Jesus himself: the blind receive sight; the lame are healed; the dumb speak; demons are cast out; and prisoners are freed.

Agnes and the Dominicans

Raymond's biography hails Agnes as a Dominican saint from the outset, declaring in the prologue to Part I that her life is cause for rejoicing by Montepulciano, Tuscany and the Order of Preachers. Although Agnes' earliest convent experiences were with Franciscans, unnamed by Raymond, he refers to her as following the customs of Dominic, her "father-to-be". When the time came for Agnes to found a monastery in Montepulciano, where there was as yet no Dominican priory, she had a vision of three ships, bearing Augustine, Francis and Dominic. After some arguing, it is Dominic who takes her into his ship.

Nonetheless, with the permission of the diocesan bishop, the church and monastery that Agnes builds at first follows the Augustinian rule. Raymond is at pains to stress the saint's orthodoxy and when she comes to entrust the care of the monastery to the Dominicans, it is with the permission of both the bishop and the legate of the Apostolic See. At the end of her life Agnes comforts her sisters "in imitation of the blessed Dominic her father and guide",[40] and Raymond reminds his readers that the monastery remains, miraculously sustained, and offering continuing consolation.

Raymond's story is complemented by contributions from other Dominicans. There is Fra Jacopo, who became the prior in Agnes' monastery, and who provides testimony to one of the healing miracles performed after Agnes' death. And Raymond also refers to a Fra Paolo di ser Pietro of Florence, also prior of the monastery, who hears with him the story of another healing. So the Order of Preachers provides the narrator, acts as guarantor of the truth of miracles and constitutes the setting for the narrative itself.

---

[40] Ibid., p. 88.

Beata Alda (Aldobrandesca) of Siena (1249–1310) and Sienese visionaries

Although Alda of Siena is frequently listed alongside the holy women introduced above, she is notably different from them. She is not commemorated either as a religious leader or as a writer or preacher, and there do not appear to have been any calls for her canonization. After the death of her husband, Bindo Bellanti,[41] Alda became a tertiary of the Holy Humility of Mary and retreated to a small cottage near Siena where she experienced ecstasies and visions and apparently performed miracles. She subsequently became a nurse at the S. Andrea hospital, where she was tormented for being a fraud yet carried out some miraculous cures. Alda was buried at the church of S. Tommaso in Siena that belonged to the Umiliati.

There are, however, two interesting aspects to Alda's story. One is the nature of the Order that she joined (see box), and the other is her biographer.

The Umiliati

The Umiliati were one of the Orders that focused on a life of poverty, and, like the Waldensians and the Beguines, opened their doors to women. That said, their origins lay in a very male-oriented world—beginning with nobles from Lombardy who had been captured by imperial forces and taken to Germany, where they adopted grey penitential garments and developed a lifestyle focused on good works and mortification of the flesh. Once they had returned home, having taken an oath of loyalty to the emperor,

---

[41] Described in the *Italian Encyclopaedia of Biography* as "modesto, colto e religioso" (modest, well-educated and religious), he died after only seven years of marriage which left Alda childless. See <https://www.treccani.it/enciclopedia/margherita-aldobrandeschi_(Dizionario-Biografico)>, accessed 24 September 2021.

their movement remained on the fringe of religious life, and they had no fixed rule. The pope (in 1178) allowed them to live at home in humility and purity; marriage was permitted, and, a particular feature of this group, they were allowed not to take oaths or engage in litigation. Although they were not allowed to hold gatherings or preach in public, they played an important part in civic life. Perhaps unsurprisingly, given that they brought back with them new skills in improved wool production, the earliest Umiliati formed trade associations and material possessions would eventually prove to be a problem.

The first female Umiliati seem to have come from Milan. Like their male counterparts they adopted severe penitential practices, including scourging, and were active in public life. They too flourished and could afford to commission a work by Giotto (for the church of All Saints in Florence[42]) when the artist was at the height of his fame. Unlike the male Order, which was eventually suppressed by papal bull in 1571, the women's Order continued until the twentieth century.

It is doubtful whether Alda would have been remembered at all without the efforts of her biographer, Gregorio Lombardelli. Lombardelli (d. 1613) was a Dominican theologian and a prolific author. He collaborated with his schoolteacher brother Orazio in the production of edifying texts for young people[43] and is best known for his treatise defending the stigmata of Catherine of Siena, *Sommario della disputa a difesa delle sacre stimate di Santa Caterina da Siena*, written at the request of Pope Clement VIII, who hoped to put an end to the arguments between Dominicans and Franciscans on the legitimacy of Catherine as a stigmatic.

---

[42] The Ognissanti Madonna is now in the Uffizi.

[43] Including, for example, *Della perseveranza christiana, corona di tutte d'altre virtù* [On Christian perseverance, the crown of all virtues] (1578).

Between 1577 and 1590, Lombardelli wrote a series of lives of Sienese holy women and men from previous centuries.[44] His life of Alda, *Vita della beata Aldobrandesca Ponzii dei' Bellanti da Siena*, is dated 1584, while other lives include Galgano Guidotti and the Carmelite Franco Senese da Grotti, along with two women who were Dominican tertiaries, Beata Genovese da Siena and Beata Nera Tolomei. Nera Tolomei was from a well-known Sienese family and is credited with converting Giovanni Batista Tolomei (d. 1320), who also became a Dominican and was beatified and whose biography Lombardelli also wrote. Although Lombardelli did not confine himself to Dominican history, it is likely that promoting the interests of his Order was a major factor in his thinking.

Lombardelli's life of Alda sets out details of her visions, in which the Virgin Mary is central, along with Lombardelli's own reflections on his subject-matter. He describes how Alda prayed for a vision of Mary as Queen of Heaven, and saw her "in a golden garment, having on her head a crown of twelve stars, and the moon beneath her feet, and a tablet in her hand, on which was written: 'daughters, be obedient to the law of the Mother'". On another occasion, while meditating before a crucifix on Christ's Passion, Alda felt impelled to taste some blood from the Saviour's side. She then saw a single drop of blood emerging which she was able to take on her tongue.

Alda is represented in art with a nail, reflecting another occasion when she meditated on Christ's Passion and wanted to see the nails of crucifixion. She was rewarded by a vision of an angel with three bloodstained nails, one much longer than the others, representing the nail that pierced Christ's feet. Alda subsequently crafted an identical nail from a tree in her garden.[45]

---

[44] Lombardelli structures his biographies rigorously, following a pattern exemplified by Tommaso da Celano's thirteenth-century biography of Clare of Assisi.

[45] All references are to *Vita della Beata Aldobrandesca Ponzii de' Bellanti da Siena*, available online at <https://books.google.co.uk/books/about/Vita_della_beata_Aldobrandesca_Ponzii_de.html?id=y8nWcOHJyloC&redir_esc=y >, accessed 24 September 2021.

Chiara Frugoni points out that a later saint, Rita of Cascia (1381–1457), is also depicted with a thorn in her hand, a thorn which she had felt pierce her head at the height of her own meditation on the cross.[46] Frugoni suggests that this is indicative of visionaries sharing common experiences in their spiritual lives, and the common structure that Lombardelli gives to all his *vitae* leads inescapably to the same conclusion. Early in his story of Alda, for example, he describes how she was tempted by the Devil with frequent memories of marital relations. Temptation also figures in the *Vita* of Nera Tolomei, who, immediately after she has taken the habit, is tempted by the sin of lust, and similar trials beset Lombardelli's other subjects as well. In the hands of a more subtle writer, temptation early in life is seen as leading to spiritual growth and overcoming it as a step towards perfection.[47]

Conclusion

Although the holy women described in this chapter are heard almost exclusively through the voices of their biographers, and their actions interpreted by them, the *vita* form becomes increasingly sophisticated. In contrast to Lombardelli's rigid hagiographical format, the preferred instrument of the jobbing writer, the lives of Margaret of Cortona and Agnes of Montepulciano (and, to a lesser extent, Clare of Montefalco) present much more individual aspects of the saints. At the same time, they reveal in various ways the motivation of the writers themselves, which will be discussed in more detail in Chapter 9.

---

[46] "Female mystics, visions and iconography", in D. Bornstein and R. Rusconi (eds), *Women and Religion in Medieval and Renaissance Italy* (Chicago: University of Chicago Press, 1996), pp. 130–64, here at p. 134.

[47] Raymond of Capua observes à propos of a very minor "cooling of fervour" on the part of Catherine, "Wisdom . . . sometimes permits his very saints to sink low by their frailties, that they may react all the more strongly, live for the future all the more watchfully, soar towards the pitch of perfection all the more eagerly and earnestly, and win the victory at last over the Enemy of our race all the more gloriously." *The Life of Catherine of Siena* (Dublin: Dominicana Publications, 1980), p. 40.

CHAPTER 4

Saints with their own voices: Umiltà of Faenza and Angela of Foligno

Written records of the teaching and meditations of the saints themselves would appear to be of paramount importance in considering the nature of their holiness. While Clare of Montefalco's voice lives on thanks only to a few particularly striking sayings that stuck in the minds of her followers, we have much greater access to the thinking of some holy women, from Clare of Assisi to Catherine of Siena, as a result of their writing or dictated work. This, of course, does not rule out interference: scribes do not always understand what they are writing down; and editors, for their own reasons, may be selective in their use of texts.

However, without Umiltà of Faenza's *Sermoni* and Angela of Foligno's *Libro*, the reputations of both women would most likely have rested solely on other people's interpretation of their mystical practices and occasional adventures. As it is, with the presence of the saints' own voices, their spirituality is revealed alongside their action, and any suggestion that they might be the stuff of myth falls away.

The saint who got away: Umiltà of Faenza (1226–1310)

Non c'è notte per chi ama (S. Umiltà Sermone 5)
[It is not night for the one who loves]
Inscription on altar stone, Chapel of
S. Umiltà, Faenza Cathedral

The life of Umiltà of Faenza is hard to uncover, not least because her several biographers differ in significant details. Faenza, a small town some sixty kilometres from Bologna, is best known for its subsequent ceramic industry, and reveals little of its own saint, beyond a small side chapel dedicated to her in the cathedral. Her companion, one Margherita (see below), is also notable by her absence. A local history guide notes a little sorrowfully that the only worthwhile representation of Umiltà (a polyptych by Pietro Lorenzetti) remains mostly in the Uffizi in Florence, the city where Umiltà spent most of her life and where she was buried.

Portrayed in Faenza holding a large book in front of her, Umiltà was particularly noted for her intellect. Yet, as Adele Simonetti notes, hers is a multifaceted story, as she was in turn a married woman, a hermit and a founder of a convent, all of which testified to "the richness of the lives of women penitents in the final centuries of the Middle Ages".[1] Indeed, her story contains many of the elements that become characteristic of the Italian holy women in general.

Escaping from marriage

There was no conversion experience for Umiltà. Born Rosanese Negusanti, she grew up in a wealthy family and had a vocation to the religious life since early childhood. She seems to have been a fabled beauty, who (like the young Catherine of Siena) spent much time in prayer and gave generously to the poor without her parents' knowledge. As a young teenager she first avoided marriage to a relative, possibly a cousin, of Emperor Frederick II, who had captured Faenza after a long siege. Rosanese's claim that she wanted only Christ as her husband was enough to discourage her suitor, but after the death of her father a couple of years later she had no choice but to marry. With her husband, Ugolotto Caccianemici, Rosanese had two children who died in infancy. The couple's lives changed when Ugolotto was diagnosed with a potentially fatal illness, possibly venereal disease, and was ordered to abstain from

---

[1]   Adele Simonetti, *I sermoni di Umiltà da Faenza. Studio e edizione* (Centro italiano di studi sull'alto medioevo, 1995), p. xi.

sex. According to Rosanese's fourteenth-century male biographers,[2] it was Ugolotto who declared he would live chastely and persuaded his wife to do the same, although it is more likely that Rosanese saw this as an answer to her prayers and the long-awaited chance to enter the religious life.

In due course, Ugolotto allowed her to leave him and enter the convent associated with the Cluniac monastery of S. Perpetua near Faenza, where she took the name of Umiltà. It is suggested that he too joined a religious Order associated with the same monastery.

Escape from the convent

Having first avoided and then escaped marriage, albeit in a somewhat unconventional way, Umiltà, by now in her mid-twenties, was free to pursue her vocation. As she settled into her new way of life, with the usual obligations of obedience and abstinence, she began to read Latin (thanks either to a human teacher or, it is said, to divine intervention), and dictated her *Sermoni*.

Biographers differ as to the order of events, but common to all of them is the story of Umiltà's second great escape. One night, following the prompting of a mysterious voice, Umiltà slipped away from S. Perpetua, climbing over a high wall in the process, and miraculously walking across the river Lamone without getting her feet wet. As for the mysterious voice: in one account it is the Virgin Mary, calling Umiltà to found the community of Santa Maria Novella near Faenza; in another it is St John the Evangelist, summoning her to found a Vallombrosan house for women in Florence, which she did, though many years later.

Seeking a still more solitary life, Umiltà moved into a cell that was constructed next to the Vallombrosan monastery of S. Apollinare where she spent a number of years as an anchorite, apparently inspiring a number

---

2   Fr Biagio (tr. E. Petroff), *The Analects of St Umiltà* in *Consolation of the Blessed* (New York: Alta Gaia Society, 1979), pp. 137–50, originally published in Latin, and Silvestro Ardenti, *Vita della beata Umiltà Faentina* (reproduction of unedited text, Imola, 1849), published in the Tuscan dialect in 1345. Two later lives, by Ignazio Guiducci in 1632 and Vincenzo Nannini in 1722, claim to follow three sources: two in Latin and one in the vernacular. References below are to Ardenti's *Vita*.

of other young women to do the same. Several details are striking from that period. The first is that Umiltà's only companion in her sealed cell was a pet weasel that only left her when she was released. The second, in keeping with the male-oriented tone of her biographers, is that her husband, hearing that she had joined the Vallombrosans, also became a member of that Order.

The Vallombrosans

The story of the Vallombrosan monks prefigures the later divisions among the Franciscans. Their Order was founded in the 1030s by a Benedictine monk, one Giovanni Gualberto, known as "the merciful knight", who built a monastery at Vallombrosa, on the slopes of Monte Secchieta, some twenty-five kilometres east of Florence. Like the Spiritual Franciscans after him, Gualberto sought a more austere, more "perfect" way of life than his Order prescribed, but without making a complete break from the Benedictines: his monks followed the Benedictine Rule with severe penalties for anyone straying from it. The Vallombrosan Order soon spread throughout Italy and more widely in Europe, where they were known as the Black Benedictines.

Gualberto's choice of an alternative lifestyle may have owed something to his earlier experience of Church institutions. He had previously been expelled from the S. Trinità monastery in Florence for *un uso eccessivo e degenerate della lettura, che gli avrebbe ispirato pratiche negromantiche e frequentazione diaboliche di donne* ("a degenerate passion for books which led him into necromancy and wicked frequenting of women"), a charge which Simonetti considers improbable, but one which is not unknown in late ancient hagiography.[3] Once reinstated, Gualberto opted instead for a different life of poverty and solitude, a preference which may well have been the cause of his fall from favour in the first place.

---

[3]   Adele Simonetti, "Santità feminile vallombrosana fra due e trecento", in Giordano Monzio Compagnoni (ed.), *L'ordo vallombrosae tra XII e XIII secolo* (Edizioni Vallombrosa, 1999), pp. 467–81, here at pp. 474–5.

Umiltà as abbess

In due course, the Vallombrosans decided that Umiltà and her companion Margaret should be admitted to their Order and that Umiltà should be their abbess. True to her vows, Umiltà obeyed. The Order may, of course, have had an ulterior motive. There would, after all, have been a limit to the number of cells they could construct for women who also wanted to live as anchorites, quite apart from any heretical beliefs they might form in their isolation. Far better to regularize the situation and bring them together in a monastic life in their own building, where their practices could be brought into line.

In 1281, Umiltà's convent got caught up in the conflict between Guelfs and Ghibellines and the sisters moved to Florence. Showing the same physical fortitude that had enabled her to scale a convent wall years before, Umiltà led the way in building a new convent,[4] which would be dedicated to her favourite saint, St John the Evangelist.

During the last thirty years of her life, Umiltà, now a Tuscan holy woman, seems to have been the focus for many miracles, which included various forms of miraculous feeding, along with healing, both of herself and of others. By contrast, it is entirely likely that her biographers chose to play down her extreme ascetic practices, preferring to highlight her life of monastic obedience, although the interest in food and feeding may reflect Umiltà's personal preoccupation.

Her companion: Margaret of Faenza (?1230–1330)

Unusually among the holy women, Umiltà had a companion who was also responsible for some texts of her own and who appears to have been beatified, although at least one scholar has doubted her very existence. We know nothing of the early life of Margherita da Faenza, who may, like Umiltà, have been of noble birth: she was a Vallombrosan nun in Umiltà's convent of S. Perpetua in Faenza, and was among those who accompanied Umiltà to Florence. After Umiltà's death, she may have succeeded her as abbess at S. Maria Novella della Malta, although this is far from certain.

---

[4]   Lorenzetti pictures her collecting stones (from the Mugnone river, a tributary of the Arno) and loading them onto a donkey.

Two versions of Margaret's life appeared very soon after her death.[5] Like the *vitae* of Umiltà, these texts include some details of the two women's mystical experiences, and of miracles associated with them, but, as Simonetti has pointed out, it is the monastic aspects of their lives that are particularly highlighted—a factor very much in keeping with the Church's desire for orthodoxy.[6]

In Lorenzetti's polyptych, Margaret is portrayed as a tiny figure at the feet of Umiltà, which effectively denies her the right to be remembered as an independent figure.

In her own words: The "sermons"

Elizabeth Petroff sees Umiltà as someone who broke the rules, which ties in nicely with her breaking away from married life and from life in a convent that was not to her liking. In the threefold disadvantage that she suffered as a woman:

> [N]ot only had she learned to read as an adult, she wrote and delivered sermons in Latin—a male language—and preached on doctrine—male territory. Her biographer sees this as evidence of a miracle.[7]

In fact, "sermons" is something of a misnomer for much of Umiltà's writing. Simonetti suggests that they reflect the new genre of *revelationes*—accounts of conversations with God, Jesus or other figures.[8] In this respect, in her dialogues Umiltà shows a marked preference for St John the Evangelist and four of her fifteen *sermoni* are in the form of conversation with him. But there are also hymns to the Virgin, prayers

---

[5] *Revelations* by Giovanni di Michaele, who claimed to be Margaret's nephew and to have received the text directly from her; and *Notabilia* by Fra Pietro da Firenze, a life written at the request of the abbess and nuns of St John the Evangelist. He claimed to have known Margaret since childhood and also that she herself dictated the work.

[6] Adele Simonetti, n. 3 above, p. 481.

[7] N. 2 above, p. 138.

[8] *I sermoni*, n. 1 above, p. lxvi.

and other conversations. These include a challenge to the archangel Gabriel: "why did you say 'blessed are you among women [*inter mulieres*]' and not 'blessed are you above all men [*super ommes viros*]'?",[9] which may have given her probable monastic audience pause for thought.

Umiltà is particularly fond of angels, both named and unnamed.[10] Indeed, her *sermoni* have been presumed to have been given her directly either by God or by an angel, although that may well have been an over-ready assumption on the part of those who chose to disregard her own scholarly abilities. She declares that she has been given two guardian angels, whom, thanks to St John, she is able to name as Sapiel ("Wisdom") and Emmanuel, the latter being from "the Angelic Order of Cherubim". Emmanuel's task was to support her in the "guardianship of [her] flock". In *Sermo XI*, she describes them as "*angeli mei dulcissimi*" (my sweetest angels), using terms that other mystics might reserve for Jesus himself, although they are also sturdy rocks, her robust protectors.[11]

She also appeals to her angels to keep her focused on her devotions and to act as mediators, freely intermingling the practical with the mystics' language of love:

> . . . walk forth in all my paths and diligently keep vigil lest enemies be strong enough to approach the doors of my heart . . . Sharpen my tongue with a keen knife for rooting up whatever vices are there and planning virtues. Place two seals of love upon my eyes, so they may be unable to look upon anything of this world as upon my Beloved; nonetheless keep these same eyes open and watchful that they be not impeded by sleep in reciting the Divine Office nor burden the mind when it ought to give

---

[9] *I sermoni (Sermo III)*, p. 28. (The page references to *I sermoni* relate to Simonetti's Latin edition.)

[10] Steven Chase claims that "few saints of the church have had as personal or as intimate a relation with angels as Saint Umiltà" and notes the significance of the name Emmanuel ("God with us"). Steven Chase, *Angelic Spirituality: Medieval Perspectives on the Ways of Angels* (New York: Paulist Press, 2002), p. 147.

[11] *I sermoni (Sermo XI)*, pp. 150, 151.

attention to praising God . . . Pray to the Eternal Word that he
may wish to draw my heart to Him and never allow it to go astray
with anyone else.[12]

While Umiltà's language has various biblical echoes, and she refers
frequently to Gospel characters, direct quotation is rarely her style,
although in *Sermo VII* she cites John 14:9-10 as an illustration of Christ's
divine authority, and Luke 1:35 and 4:1 as evidence of the Holy Spirit
being with Mary and Jesus respectively.[13] Perhaps her knowledge of
scripture did not extend far beyond the Gospels. For example, in her
sermon on the holy angels (*Sermo IV*) she refers to Emmanuel being
baptized in "that royal river that always flows forth from the throne of
the most high, in which the exalted God, the Father, remains, and the Son
and the Spirit, who flames forth", an apparent reference to Revelation 22:1
and the river of the water of life, although there it is God and the Lamb
who are enthroned rather than the Trinity. She continues, "The rivers,
of which there are five, are greater than all seas—and over each river in
its great magnitude, God, the most high remains seated. The rivers, of
which there are four major ones, all flow to the sea",[14] which seems to
reflect the river that flowed out of Eden (Genesis 2:10) and divided into
four branches. But the exact references are unimportant. Umiltà's aim is
to convey the wonder of the surroundings in which *her* angel is set, since
"she is in the glory of God and serves as interpreter of the dominion and
power descending from the greatest heights".

When she is not in conversation with the divine, Umiltà's writing
veers between the didactic and the mystical, which may have suited
the Vallombrosan sisters and brothers for whom it was destined. This
is reflected in *Sermo IX* where instructions to her listeners lead into a
hymn to the Virgin, which intermingles verse and prose.[15] Simonetti's
conclusion is that her life offers a model of saintliness, albeit one that
was linked to a form of traditional monasticism that was destined to be

---

[12] Ibid., p. 152.

[13] *I sermoni (Sermo VII)*, p. 85.

[14] *I sermoni (Sermo IV)*, p. 42.

[15] *I sermoni*, pp. 107–33.

overshadowed by the continued expansion of the mendicant Orders.[16] This may well explain why only a few copies of her *vitae* appear to have existed, with the *Sermoni* themselves being of interest to only a few.

A model of holiness

Umiltà's story is rich in traditional elements, both religious and secular. Her noble birth, accomplishments and refusal of marriage are all recurrent themes in the tradition of hagiography. There is, too, the fairy-tale presence of the weasel: a creature related to the stoat whose white fur (ermine) had long been a symbol of purity. And while the later Middle Ages saw the emergence of a new ideal of a female religious—one who engaged in energetic action on behalf of her Order and the wider Church—Umiltà for the most part represents the more traditional model, of a life spent in solitary mystical pursuits.

In the absence of eye-catching public events, Silvestro Ardenti includes instead some occasional inexplicable features to indicate the holiness of Umiltà. On one unspecified occasion, when Umiltà was weeping over Christ's suffering, her tears suddenly turned to blood, a phenomenon she was quick to conceal with her handkerchief.[17] Ardenti describes all this in a single sentence without further comment, which constitutes one chapter in his biography. By contrast, he devotes an unusually long chapter to a description of her first resting place, a stone tomb which unaccountably began to emit the "most pure and clear" oil.[18] There is some discussion among onlookers as to whether there might be a mundane explanation, but the testimony of visiting monks and a much revered older nun declares this to be a sign of holiness, and, in the presence of the Bishop of Florence, the saint's body is eventually moved with some ceremony to a more exalted place.

It is also notable that many of the miracles associated with both Umiltà and her companion Margaret work for the benefit of themselves or their Order. Stories of miraculous feeding (see Chapter 8 below) are not destined to improve the lot of the local poor. Umiltà's story in

---

[16] Ibid., p. xxx.

[17] Ardenti, *Vita*, p. 41.

[18] Ibid., pp. 55–7.

particular is one of a free spirit ultimately bound by the constraints of a religious community, clearly symbolized by the presence of Margaret. Her biographers play down the mystical in favour of the disciplined monastic life that they seek to uphold.

Umiltà's acceptance of her monastic role is reinforced by her *sermoni* in which she exhorts her sisters and brothers to pursue a virtuous life, without drawing overmuch on her own experiences. Yet her *vita* has little to say about her undoubted intellectual abilities. Ardenti describes a visit to her cell by the Bishop of Faenza who greatly appreciates her "devout words and holy preaching" (*devote parole e sante orazioni*),[19] which is his only direct reference to her skills as attested by an authority of the Church. However, Ardenti does have a couple of mystical experiences to draw on. There was the occasion when Umiltà was dictating *certi trattati* ("certain tracts") to one of her sisters and two others noticed a white dove with golden feet and a golden beak apparently whispering in her ear as she spoke. Umiltà confirmed that this was the case but swore her sisters to secrecy during her lifetime. Ardenti notes in passing that Umiltà wrote *El libro degli angeli e dell'anima* (Book of angels and of the soul) and was responsible for many holy sermons (*santi sermoni*).[20]

Then, during Umiltà's early days in the monastery, her sisters had had the unnerving experience of hearing her read from an unspecified book "things that they had never heard before" (*cose non mai udite*).[21] Since her words are understood to be prompted by the Holy Spirit, there is no suggestion by Ardenti that this is indicative of a special intellectual gift, although it would seem likely that this is what is being symbolized. However, Lorenzetti's inclusion of the episode, depicting Umiltà reading to her sisters at a meal, ensures that this interpretation remains a possibility. It is also possible that Umiltà dictating her work is the subject of a missing panel.

Like Margaret of Cortona and Catherine of Siena, Umiltà's reputation is closely linked to that of her region. Most obviously, the visit from the Bishop of Faenza serves to strengthen the renown of both bishop

---

[19]   Ibid., p. 23.

[20]   Ibid., pp. 41–2.

[21]   Ibid., p. 10.

and holy woman, and to promote the town of Faenza itself. There is a strange little story, most probably of popular origin, in which Umiltà responds to the fear of her sisters when the whole region is affected by a dangerous snowfall. Umiltà raises her eyes to heaven, whereupon the sun appears and the snow stops. Unsurprisingly, danger is averted both for her community and the whole "*contrada*", although that wider benefit remains an apparently secondary concern.[22]

Similarly, local people receive incidental benefit when Umiltà foresees a famine affecting all of Tuscany and sends her representative to Florence to obtain the necessary provisions for the coming year. The famine duly comes to pass, causing many deaths across the province. But Umiltà's monastery is unaffected and, notes Ardenti, "many people received help".[23]

Lorenzetti's polyptych

Umiltà probably owes much of her enduring reputation not to her own words but to the work of one artist. Over a long period, between 1313 and 1348, the Sienese artist Pietro Lorenzetti worked on an altarpiece depicting Umiltà's life and miracles. The central figure, which was originally flanked by sixteen panels,[24] is wearing a sheepskin cap (a symbol of the saint's rejection of more attractive clothing). She holds a book in her left hand, and in her right what looks at first sight to be a quill but is actually a flail, emphasizing her penitential practices.

Despite being credited with introducing naturalism into Sienese art, Lorenzetti painted an altarpiece that was very much old style. Luke Syson comments on a "culture of imitation" that was central both to continuing Siena's artistic tradition into the next century and to upholding the collective identity of civic and religious groups:

---

[22] Ibid., p. 31.

[23] Ibid., p. 51.

[24] With the exception of two panels that are in Berlin's Gemäldegalerie, the polyptych with its surviving panels is now housed in the Uffizi in Florence.

The polyptych altarpieces painted for the churches and chapels of
the preaching and penitential orders, and for the meeting places
of the lay confraternities linked to them, are prime examples of
these deliberately conservative commissions . . .

A crucial component of the mission of the urban mendicant
orders . . . was their interaction with a lay public. Their insistence
upon aesthetic orthodoxy should be linked with their need to
speak in a language that was shared and familiar.[25]

Besides situating Umiltà firmly in an orthodox tradition of holiness,
Lorenzetti's work also establishes the key elements in her life and
character that are to be remembered, including the flight from the
monastery, reading and preaching to her sisters and sharing in physical
building work.

The conservative conceptualizing of Umiltà is consistent across
biography (Simonetti argues that she is presented as a hagiographic
model in her own lifetime, endowed with traditional hagiographic
features[26]), art and, indeed, her own writing and teaching. Despite
Umiltà's Vallombrosan pedigree, or perhaps because of it, her *sermoni*
tend for the most part to focus the reader's attention on the orthodoxy
of her beliefs. The saint who got away never quite succeeded in escaping
the clutches of the mother Church.

The pilgrim who created a rumpus: Angela of Foligno (?1248–1309)

In 1291, Angela, a newly professed Third Order Franciscan, made a
pilgrimage from the trading town of Foligno in eastern Umbria to Assisi,
a distance of some sixteen kilometres. The purpose of her pilgrimage,
according to her later account, was to pray to Francis that she might keep

---

[25]   Luke Syson et al., *Renaissance Siena: Art for a City* (London: National Gallery
       Company Limited, 2007), pp. 44–5.

[26]   *I sermoni,* p. xvii.

the rule of her Order, that she might know Christ's presence and that she might become and remain truly poor.

Angela's journey took her through the ancient hill town of Spello, where the surrounding countryside and, in particular, Monte Subasio is said to have been the inspiration for St Francis' Canticle of Creation. Here, conscious no doubt of following in the footsteps of her beloved saint, Angela was filled with a sense of awareness of the presence of the Holy Spirit. And at the point where her path met the road going up to Assisi, Angela entered into a prolonged religious experience, later described in her *Memoriale*, where the Holy Spirit not only spoke to her but promised to keep talking to her as she continued her journey. Angela's companions were unaware what was going on, and nothing outwardly untoward happened until they reached Assisi and paid a visit to the Basilica of St Francis.

The Holy Spirit promised Angela not to leave her until, after having had her supper, she returned to the church for a second time. As she did so, Angela had a vision of St Francis held in the arms of Christ, and heard the Spirit say to her, "I will hold you this closely, even closer than the eyes of the body can see." Then the Spirit left her, or, as Angela put it, her "consolation" was withdrawn from her.

This withdrawal brought Angela to public attention in a dramatic way. In the sight of a large number of people, at the entrance to the church, Angela started to screech loudly and incomprehensibly. Later she declared that her words had been "Love unknown, why do you leave me?" but that they were covered by her screams. Unsurprisingly, this was a source of some embarrassment to those who knew her, and particularly for her confessor (and subsequently her scribe), Brother Arnaldo, who was also related to her. He wrote this:

> My pride and embarrassment were so great that I waited indignantly at a distance for her to finish making these noises. And when she finished screeching, she got up from the entrance and approached me. I could hardly speak to her calmly. I told her she should never again dare to come to Assisi, where such evil

was possessing her; I also told her companions never to bring her there again.[27, 28]

Angela's spiritual journey hitherto had more in common with the English mystic Margery Kempe (c. 1373-1438), whose ecstatic outbursts also led to her rejection by her fellow travellers to the Holy Land, than with her compatriots. Angela was converted to an active faith in God at the age of thirty-seven, which compared with other mystics is relatively late in life, and perhaps because of her maturity she did not generally indulge in the extreme behaviour that characterized Margaret of Cortona or Catherine of Siena. She lived longer than many mystics as well—a likely consequence of not subjecting her body to deprivation and near starvation. There is a hint of the reason for this in her recollection of the Holy Spirit's words to her on her return journey from Assisi: "Your entire life: your eating, drinking, sleeping—every aspect of your life—is pleasing to me."[29]

Angela was born in Foligno in or around 1248. As would be the case with Catherine of Siena and other Sienese saints, her birthplace is significant. Foligno lay on the Via Flaminia, the trading route that linked Rimini on the Adriatic coast with Rome, at a point where the road divided and branched off to Assisi. Like the citizens of Siena who owed much to the Via Francigena, the pilgrim route that ran from Canterbury to Rome, the people of Foligno were very well placed to absorb news of political and religious movements from passing travellers. In addition, Foligno's proximity to Assisi meant that the activities of Francis of Assisi, Clare of Assisi and their fast-growing communities were already well known there. The Franciscan Order had been founded in 1209 and expanded rapidly, while there were communities of Poor Clares at both

---

[27] Unless otherwise indicated, the English translation of the *Memoriale* is that by John Cirigano (1990) and used in Cristina Mazzoni (ed.), *Angela of Foligno: Memorial* (Woodbridge: Boydell and Brewer, 1999). Quotations from *Il Libro* are from the edition by Salvatore Aliquò and Sergio Andreoli (Rome: Città Nuova, 2009); the translations from that are my own.

[28] Mazzoni, *Angela of Foligno*, p. 37.

[29] Ibid., p. 44.

Foligno and Spello from around 1218. So Angela was from the moment of her conversion caught up in a network of new religious ideas and a developing movement of holy women.

When Angela was in her early twenties, she married and raised a family. By her own admission she (again like Margery Kempe) appears to have enjoyed the good things of life. Her eventual conversion would fill her with contrition about her previous lifestyle, which she describes in terms of "fine foods, fancy clothing and head-dresses". In her *Memoriale*, there is a hint of sexual misbehaviour, when, in echoes of Margaret of Cortona, she refers to being forgiven like Mary Magdalene.

Unsurprisingly, Angela's conversion led to her growing alienation from her family. Shockingly, perhaps, she prayed for God to release her from them, and still more shockingly within a couple of years her husband and children were all dead, which she attributes to God's will:

> I was still with my husband—and so there was bitterness when I was spoken to or treated unjustly; nevertheless, I endured as patiently as I could. And then in accordance with God's will, my mother died; she had been a great hindrance to me. Later, my husband and all my children died within a short time. And because I had already begun the way of the cross and had asked God that they should die, I felt a deep consolation following their deaths. I knew that God had accomplished these things for me, and that my heart would always be in God's heart and God's heart would always be in mine.[30]

Such an apparent answer to prayer led her to sell all the family wealth.

Angela understood, therefore, what it meant to renounce a life of plenty for material poverty and at the same time to move from spiritual aridness to spiritual riches. More importantly for her writing, though, she knew all about marital love and maybe about the lure of extramarital love as well. So when she writes of her love for God, we know that she has a human yardstick by which she can measure it. While writers such as Catherine of Siena express their feelings for God in words that echo

---

[30]   Ibid., pp. 26-7.

the passionate sexuality of medieval secular poetry, Angela's sometimes quite explicit language of divine love is made more realistic by her own experience. Her *Memoriale* speaks of "the burning fire and pleasure of love when Christ is in my soul" and goes on to refer to "such a fire in the three shameful parts that I used to apply a hot flame to them, in order to extinguish that other fire", at which point her embarrassed scribe changes the subject.[31]

The Franciscan Third Order gave Angela a spirituality centred on poverty which she could make her own. As Mazzoni comments, "[p]overty was for Angela a worldly reflection of our human condition with respect to God, a condition fully assumed by Christ himself through the incarnation."[32] And equally importantly, the Order gave her access to spiritual advisors and a ready-made community of like-minded people. In this environment, Angela quickly built up her own following of ordained men and lay people, to whom she in turn was to become a spiritual guide and mother.[33]

Indeed, following the excitement in Assisi, little more is heard of Angela, at least as far as a wider public is concerned. After she had dictated an account of her experiences to Brother Arnaldo in a memoir (the *Memoriale*), she seems to have become a spiritual guide to local Franciscans, referred to in her later writings as her sons (*figli*). Her letters to them were collected together under the general heading of *Instructiones* and form Parts 2 and 3 of her "book"—*Il Libro*—with the *Memoriale* now forming Part 1.

After her death, Angela's body was preserved in the church of S. Francesco in Foligno. Despite reports of miracles performed at her tomb she was not canonized for another 700 years, although she remained

---

[31] Ibid., pp. 51, 66.

[32] Ibid., p. 2.

[33] In her preface to the *Complete Works of Angela of Foligno*, tr. Paul Lachance, (New York: Paulist Press, 1993), Romana Guarnieri questions how Angela might have become familiar with writings such as the *Testament of Saint Francis* (1226) or St Bonaventure's *The Soul's Journey into God* (1259) which are reflected in her writing, concluding that she may have heard them as part of the Church's liturgy or through popularized versions.

the object of local veneration and was often referred to as a saint. Her reputation seems to have been overshadowed by the veneration of Francis and Clare of Assisi. Unlike Catherine of Siena, she was not destined to become the patron saint of her hometown, which remains dedicated to S. Feliciano, a third-century bishop and martyr. Angela was beatified in 1701 by Pope Clement XI, who was himself born in Umbria. She became widely known as *Magistra Theologorum* ("Mistress of Theologians"), a title that apparently originated with her contemporaries but was perpetuated by the seventeenth-century Dutch Jesuit theologian, Maximilian Sandaeus. The appropriateness of this designation was endorsed by Pope John Paul II, who, in June 1993, visited Foligno and prayed at the altar in San Francesco where Angela's remains lie.

At the start of 2013, Pope Benedict XVI promised that Angela would become a saint by means of a papal declaration ("equivalent canonization") rather than through the classic route of canonization, thereby reflecting the long-standing veneration of her by significant Church figures. Pope Francis kept this promise and Angela was canonized on 9 October that same year.

Angela in her own words

Her scribe

Brother Arnaldo, who translated into Latin what Angela dictated in her Umbrian dialect, appears to be a much more human figure, with less ecclesiastical baggage, than Margaret's Fra Giunta. In the *Memoriale*, he comes across as a faithful translator and scribe and, unlike Catherine of Siena's scribe and mentor Raymond of Capua, he has no hagiographic agenda. As the passage already quoted suggests, Arnaldo is not always comfortable with his role or with the sentiments that Angela expresses. But thanks to him and his regular interventions, the *Memoriale* is written in a straightforward and appealing style, which contrasts markedly with Angela's own more didactic style in Parts 2 and 3 of *Il Libro*.

Arnaldo never uses Angela's name, preferring to refer to her as "Christ's faithful one" (*la fedele di Cristo*). Nor does he name their native Foligno, perhaps wishing to protect his own identity. Yet despite his initial embarrassment at Angela's outburst in Assisi, Arnaldo comes to recognize her superior spiritual qualities, once he has satisfied himself that she is not possessed by an evil spirit. He refers modestly to himself as receiving "special grace from God [that] enabled me to write very reverently and to fear adding any statement of my own, but only to write what I could grasp while she was speaking".[34] Arnaldo occasionally asks for clarification, trying, for instance, to establish whether Angela was hearing the voice of Christ or the Holy Spirit. However, once the narrative moves on from the events that Arnaldo witnessed and tried to make sense of, his role is to introduce other spiritual experiences, which he often does by addressing his fellow scribes (*frate scrittore*) and explaining how he got Angela to tell him about them. In so doing, he reveals himself as having an eye for a good story.

Part 1 of *Il Libro: Memoriale*

Angela's *Memoriale* sets her Assisi experience and other ecstatic moments into the wider context of her spiritual development. Like other mystics she describes her spiritual life in terms of the soul's progress or "steps". It seems that she had thirty such steps in mind, but after the first nineteen Brother Arnaldo gives up and groups the remainder into seven "supplementary steps" on the grounds that he is unable to distinguish further between them. Unlike those medieval mystics who typically distinguished just seven steps that represent the soul's way to perfection, Angela saw her steps as representing changes made by the soul as it proceeds along the path of penitence. So Angela's first step is her awareness of her own sin, which is manifested in better crying, while her final step is to come into the presence of God, the "All Good" (*Ogni Bene*), the God whom unusually she encounters in darkness.

Angela's spirituality as it emerges from the *Memoriale* is focused on the physical body of Christ, and therefore also on the Eucharist, and on God who is all loving, all good, all powerful, whom she also perceives as an essentially physical being. In her vision of Christ in the Eucharist, her gaze is drawn to his neck and throat, which produces in her a joy that

---

34 Mazzoni, *Angela of Foligno*, p. 38.

she says has never left her.[35] Similarly, she perceives the eyes of God, a revelation which again produces in her a happiness that she believes no saint before her has described.[36]

In her final step, Angela encounters the mystery of the Trinity, and again her description is very physical. She sees herself as somehow standing or lying in the midst of the Trinity. The words of Christ she hears have a Johannine ring: "You are me and I am you", and she is led to a certainty that she articulates in a song of praise of striking intimacy:[37]

> I praise you God, my delight,
> in your cross I have laid my bed.

In the course of this final section, we also learn of Angela's encounter with St Francis on a subsequent visit to Assisi, revealing her devotion to the founder of her Order, and an intimacy that will be echoed in Catherine of Siena's vision of Francis and St Dominic, when she was pondering which Order she should join. Francis addresses Angela as "light, daughter of Light, who is light of all light", and the saint continues to talk to her throughout her ten-day stay in the town.

Throughout the *Memoriale,* Brother Arnaldo's questions of clarification, and his frequent comments on what he is hearing from Angela, make the text unusually accessible. The overall impression is of Angela's delight in the humanity of Jesus, a delight which spills over towards the other Persons of the Trinity, presented to us in a strikingly human way.

Parts 2 and 3 of *Il Libro: Instructiones*

The *Memoriale* represents around half of Angela's book. The remaining sections bring together letters and other writings that instruct, train and encourage her spiritual "sons". For the most part Brother Arnaldo is now absent, his task passed to other scribes, so the reader no longer has an appealing intermediary to clarify and structure Angela's thoughts.

---

[35]   *Il Libro*, p. 63.

[36]   Ibid., p. 70.

[37]   Ibid., p. 137.

Some of these pieces are short, even fragmentary, while others are longer meditations. There are letters which have a clear pastoral intent, offering comfort in time of spiritual need. There is the occasional longer didactic piece of writing, such as "The duty to love God" (*Il dovere di amare Dio*). In this, Angela's tendency to list abstract terms detracts somewhat from her readability. She distinguishes three types of poverty which is itself one of three elements characterizing the life of Christ (voluntary poverty, being held in contempt, and the most intense suffering). Yet while rhetorical devices abound, there remains a certain simplicity of expression and appeal to the emotions that is reminiscent of the *Memoriale*.

Throughout *Il Libro*, Franciscan values of poverty and humility find frequent expression, alongside theological reflections on such great themes as the cross and the Trinity. The Franciscan connection ensured that Angela's writings not only survived but became known much more widely. And that, coupled with Angela's own particular spiritual experiences, meant that their influence on other holy women of the medieval period was assured.

Angela in art

Angela has not been the subject of great art or well-known artists, and only rarely does she appear among various saints in works with a different religious focus. This may be attributed both to Angela's low profile and to a lack of artistic activity in Foligno itself around the time of her death.

From the seventeenth century onwards, however, there are various artworks featuring Angela by unknown local artists. A seventeenth-century painting in the Convento di San Francesco in Foligno shows Angela holding a large cross against the left side of her body, while her arms are full of instruments of the Passion of Christ—large nails, a scourge and so on. The artist has also given her a "rayed" halo (*aureola raggiata*) despite the fact that she had not yet been canonized.[38] Given

---

[38] Both this, and the more conventional halo, are common in pictures of Angela from the time of her death onwards, reinforcing the local conviction of her sanctity.

the centrality of the cross in Angela's writing, it is not surprising that the cross and crucifixion should feature largely in depictions of her. However, the instruments and symbols of the Passion, which became part of Angela's iconography from about this time, are not much found in earlier portrayals of saints. It has been suggested that this iconography, "typical of Counter-Reformation piety", has emerged as a result of the story of Clare of Montefalco (see Chapter 3 above), whose heart was found after her death to contain miniature versions of such instruments.[39]

Almost a century after Angela's beatification, a recently appointed Bishop of Foligno, Filippo Trenta (1785–96), commissioned three altarpieces from the Bolognese artist Gaetano Gandolfi. Gandolfi was a successful and prolific artist whose early works reflect the late Baroque style. By the time of the Foligno commission, however, Gandolfi was already well into middle age and painting in a neoclassical style. Of the three pieces that arrived around 1791, one, an annunciation, is now lost. The others were a piece commissioned for the high altar in S. Feliciano Cathedral—*San Feliciano liberates Foligno from the plague*[40]—and one depicting Angela in ecstasy. This was commissioned for the altar of Beata Angela, where it remains today.

While the subject of the painting is Angela's vision of the Christ child, the work is also a statement of her spirituality. Angela, dressed as a Franciscan tertiary, receives the somewhat distant baby's blessing, while immediately in front of her a pair of muscular angels hold out a crown of roses and a crown of thorns. Above her, cherubs struggle with an inclined cross, while diametrically opposite them, barely visible to the observer, tiny figures carry instruments of Christ's passion. In the background

---

[39]   See Maria Raffaella Trabalza, *Sante e beate umbre tra il XIII e il XIV secolo. Mostro iconografia* (Edizioni dell'Arquata, 1986), a volume compiled to mark the 700th anniversary of Angela's conversion, p. 134. The painting described appears at p. 145.

[40]   It is not uncommon for a town's patron saint to be credited with averting disaster centuries later. Margaret of Cortona was also believed to be responsible for saving her town from the plague. But while Angela was often referred to as a saint locally long before her canonization, she did not replace the town's patron S. Feliciano in this respect.

on the skyline is an outline of the town of Foligno. Angela's love for the crucified Christ is made paramount through these features, while the crown of roses also indicates her love for the Virgin Mary.

Down the centuries this well-established symbolism contributed to the cult of Angela promoted by the Franciscan Order, echoing calls for her beatification and eventual canonization.

Conclusion: The conceptualization of scholarship

With Umiltà and Angela, the idea of the mystic as scholar enters the Tuscan arena. It is not what they wrote and taught that captures the imagination of biographers and artists so much as the fact that they did it at all. And it is this that seals their reputation right up to the present day.

Reference to scholarship is made most notably by those concerned with beatification or sanctification processes, as in Angela's designation as *magistra theologorum* in 1701, or in more recent times by popes concerned to highlight the presence of women in the Church's observance (as, for example, Catherine of Siena and Bridget of Sweden being named as Doctors of the Church). In earlier iconography, it was sufficient to portray the subject holding a book to establish her intellectual and, importantly, her orthodox credentials, as with the portrait of Umiltà in Faenza and in Lorenzetti's polyptych.

The pattern of an intellectual woman had been well established in the legend of Katherine of Alexandria, who famously debated Christianity with fifty male orators. While, later, the most distinguished portrayals of Katherine in Renaissance art by Caravaggio (1598-9) and Raphael (c. 1507) would retain the traditional emphasis on the saint's martyrdom, some lesser-known works show her reading at a desk or in a chair, her wheel by her side or simply holding a book.[41]

---

[41] Of the Venetian Crivelli brothers, only Vittore depicts Katherine with both a wheel and a book (c. 1469), while Carlo produced a number of works featuring the wheel. The early sixteenth-century north Italian artist Bernadino Luini focuses on the stunningly beautiful face of Katherine who just holds a book.

Despite its small scale, Ardenti's biography of Umiltà highlights the saint's act of writing without examining anything of its content. Yet it is an act that he seems to attribute to divine inspiration through the person of the Holy Spirit rather than any innate intellectual ability, a picture which perhaps fits better with his overall portrayal of her life in community.

Ultimately, it is being part of a good story that is important. So thanks to their distinctive literary legacies Umiltà and Angela restore a dimension of scholarship to the portrayals of holy women and pave the way for the acceptance and promulgation of the best-known writer of them all, Catherine of Siena.

PART III

Catherine of Siena: The holy woman and the city

Introduction to Part III

With the arrival on the scene of Catherine of Siena, one of the great saints of the Church, the concept of a holy woman suddenly becomes much more complex. Certainly she shares with earlier holy women an intense spirituality, manifested in frequent ecstatic visions, and a devotion to ascetic practices that surely contributed to her early death. Like them she is torn between a reclusive way of living and a life of more public service. But in the case of Catherine, her public includes popes and princes, and her position in the heart of a powerful city presents very different challenges from the Tuscan hill towns of Cortona or Montepulciano.

By the late fourteenth century, portrayals of holiness had arrived at a greater maturity, as evidenced by Raymond of Capua's long and detailed biography of Catherine, which draws on family memories as well as testimonies by Church dignitaries, and which is informed by the author's very close association with the saint. But still more significant for the question of conceptualization is the work of artists, with the emergence of the Sienese school and wealthy benefactors to support them. The city too, in adopting Catherine as one of its patrons ensured that Catherine would remain associated with its fame at a key point in its history. Add to this Catherine's prolific writing—her many letters and the *Dialogo* that she dictated—which would become widely known thanks to widespread travel across Europe and the subsequent arrival of printing, and it seems that with Catherine the understanding and dissemination of the concept of a holy woman reaches its peak. The small number of Italian mystics who followed her were more widely dispersed and received little general acclaim. Catherine's influence, and indeed that of her predecessors, is seen instead in England, in the key figures of Margery Kempe and Julian of Norwich.

The chapters in this section are necessarily selective. Given the amount of scholarly (and more popular) attention paid to Catherine over 600 years, it would be foolish and presumptuous to claim fresh insights. Instead they will focus on aspects of Catherine's life that echo the experiences of her predecessors, while resulting in new challenges for the Church. And they will consider how the work of writers and artists creates an understanding of holiness that both builds on that of the saints of the past and contributes to a vibrant new tradition.

CHAPTER 5

A new model for Tuscany: Scenes
from the life of Catherine of Siena

She is a heavenly woman, an angel on earth, for her way of life is
not earthly but angelic.

William of Flete, Letter to Raymond of Capua[1]

Background

In the thirty years between the death of Agnes of Montepulciano and the
birth of Catherine of Siena, the stories of the earlier mystics had spread
across central Italy. We know that Raymond of Capua took Catherine
to visit Agnes' tomb, but otherwise there is little to link the women
physically. However, as we have seen, the earlier women, spread across
various locations, had (or were perceived to have) sufficiently similar
experiences and spirituality for a clear concept of their shared forms
of holiness to emerge. The question now is, how will the activities of
Catherine reflect and build on that foundation, as we move from the
relative isolation of the countryside to the city, with its much wider sphere
of influence? And how will the successes of previous holy women in
taking control of their lives and spirituality be repeated and surpassed
in the life of one of Italy's greatest saints?

Catherine of Siena is the unquestioned giant among Italian holy
women. Much of this is down to the woman herself, and her gifts of
writing and preaching which she exercised widely, quite apart from her

---

[1]   In Benedict Hackett, O.S.A., *William Flete, O.S.A., and Catherine of Siena*
       (Villanova, PA: Augustinian Press, 1992), p. 173.

contribution to wider society. However, it is unlikely that her reputation would have spread far beyond her native Tuscany had it not been for a number of political and cultural factors that enabled her to become the figure she still is today.

At the time of Catherine's birth in 1347, there was a certain feel-good factor evident in Siena, at least as far as the upper and middle classes were concerned. The city enjoyed considerable prosperity, thanks to the relatively new business of banking and to the flourishing cloth and wool trade. The latter had brought Catherine's father, Giacomo Benincasa, a dyer by profession, a very comfortable standard of living, which enabled him to provide well for his two dozen children. Giacomo's family was also well connected: as Thomas Luongo observes, they were "close to the highest levels of social and political power",[2] a fact that would stand the future saint in good stead when she took on a public role.

There was also an air of freedom. Along with Florence and Lucca, Siena ranked as a genuine republic of Tuscany, and for the time being there were no signs of any repressive interests trying to take power. There was also a certain intellectual freedom. For the privileged classes, as the Renaissance period dawned, the outward character of life began to change. Already, with the decline in the power of the Church, the later Middle Ages were seeing increasing secularization. This did not necessarily mean that people turned away from their Christian roots. Rather, they were more inclined to challenge them, particularly the institutions of the Church. And continuing the growing trend of the previous century, it was Christian laypeople as much as the clergy who emerged as the spiritual leaders of the time. So while Catherine accepted the discipline of the Church, she never held back from criticizing its mismanagement and those responsible for it. As a Dominican tertiary she was something of a handful, obedient to her confessor yet often losing patience with him. From her parents Catherine inherited both a strong character and a reverence for her faith, and this is evident both in her mysticism and in her determination to put her beliefs into action. Sometimes termed "active mysticism", this combination of genuine religious conviction and a

---

[2]   F. Thomas Luongo, *The Saintly Politics of Catherine of Siena* (New York: Cornell University Press, 2006), p. 30.

willingness to engage with the problems of the world remained attractive in a secularized age.

Siena was also a place of great contrasts, and these are closely reflected in the life of Catherine herself. Her happy and healthy childhood contrasted forcefully with the poverty of peasants living in the country areas around the city; and the trade honestly pursued by her father was elsewhere marred by restrictive practices. The Black Death first hit Siena in 1348 and returned in 1374, when Catherine was drawn to minister to the sick and dying. And the Sienese calm was far from typical, as the fourteenth century saw national and international conflicts, and the Church was rocked by the consequences of having a succession of popes not in Rome but in Avignon, which eventually resulted in schism—a situation on which Catherine expressed her views most forcefully. While the Renaissance brought a period of cultural development and change that is arguably without parallel in history, the years after 1350 also saw an overall economic decline in Italy, and the effects of the plague would be felt in the peninsula for the next century and a half.

The literate people of Tuscany were also aware of another crucial development. The great Florentine poet Dante Alighieri had laid the foundations for a national literary language when he raised the status of the vernacular through his poetry and prose. And he created new ways of thinking, most significantly in his *Vita Nuova* ("New Life"). This short work, dating from the early 1290s, combines prose and poetry and has as its central figure a lady who reflects the qualities of local holy women. In it, the poet turns away from the imported conventions of French and Provençal "courtly love", in which the object of the poet's affections is typically a cruel and haughty lady, and replaces them with the figure of a woman adored for her spirituality and graciousness, reminiscent of the Virgin Mary herself. And, as already indicated (Chapter 2 above), holy women were ready to adopt the language of the troubadour lover and apply it to their love for Jesus, his mother, saints and angels.

The influence of Dante and his predecessors can perhaps also be seen in Catherine's spiritual writing. The virtue of discretion was at the very heart of the ideal of love developed by the poets, and in Catherine's *Dialogo*, discretion or, better, "discernment" is a recurring theme. By the late sixteenth century, editors had divided the work into a succession of "treatises", including a lengthy "treatise on discretion". Giuliana Cavallini's 1968 edition, however, re-established the work's original more free-flowing structure, which reflects its origin in a five-day frenzy of dictation while Catherine was in ecstasy.[3]

For Catherine, *discrezione* is an attitude towards God and people which springs from humility, another great virtue common to both the Christian and secular poetic traditions. So, for example, in the *Dialogo* "her" priests are described as a people whose hearts bring to God:

> . . . the pearl of justice, which it had always kept in sight by being just to everyone and doing its duty with discernment. Therefore it offers [God] the justice of true humility . . . [4]

By contrast, the corresponding vice, indiscretion or lack of discernment, is one of the four principal vices of "trees of death", along with pride, self-love and impatience.[5]

It might also be argued, more generally, that Catherine was to a degree predisposed to literary influence. Her maternal grandfather, Nuccio Piacente,[6] was himself a poet who is chiefly remembered for an effusive sonnet addressed to the Florentine poet Guido Cavalcanti (1255–1300), who was a friend of Dante and from whom Nuccio was presumably seeking some kind of patronage.[7]

---

[3]   See Suzanne Noffke OP (tr.), *Catherine of Siena, The Dialogue* (New York: Paulist Press, 1980), Introduction, p. 15.

[4]   Ibid., p. 265.

[5]   Ibid., p. 73.

[6]   Also known as Nuccio Sanese ("the Sienese").

[7]   In the *Vita Nuova*, Dante describes Cavalcanti as his "first friend", after Dante had sent him a sonnet beginning "To every loving heart and captive soul", which evidently met with Cavalcanti's approval. *Vita Nuova*, tr. Mark Musa (Oxford: Oxford University Press, 1999), p. 7.

Catherine's Siena

Incarnate Wisdom raised up one certain wonderful young woman,
a holy maiden, in the province of Tuscany, in that city of Siena
which has been called from ancient times "the city of the Virgin".
Raymond of Capua, First Prologue to
the Life of Catherine of Siena.[8]

Catherine Benincasa grew up in a community where everyone knew
everyone else's business, down to the most intimate details of family life.
By the time she made her vow of virginity, at the age of seven, she would
have had a pretty good idea of what she was renouncing. Visitors to
the oldest parts of Siena today soon see that it could not be otherwise.
Now, as then, houses are tumbled together on the hillsides with only
the narrowest of streets to keep them apart. Catherine's home was no
different. The Benincasa family lived on a steep narrow street to the
north of the city's central piazza, the Piazza del Campo, which by 1347
was already dominated by the town hall, the Palazzo Pubblico, whose
imposing tower was completed the following year.

Communities have played an important part in the history of Siena,
with the various groupings of them proving to be long-lasting and
inspiring deep loyalties. In Tuscany, and also in Lombardy to the north,
this led to the formation of powerful city-republics and, inevitably, bitter
rivalry between them. The history of Italy itself is a story of disparate
groups and national disunity, with lasting unity coming only as a result
of nationalist pressure in the nineteenth century.

Catherine's Siena was made up of forty-two districts known as
contrade, and each was responsible for collecting taxes, maintaining order
and so on. The parish church served as an administrative headquarters for
the local mayor and his councillors. The *contrade* were in turn grouped
into three city districts (*terzi*) corresponding to the three hills on which
the city is built. Catherine's *contrada* fell within the Terzo di Camollia.

---

[8]   All references are to *The Life of Catherine of Siena* by Raymond of Capua, tr.
and ed. Conleth Kearns, 1980 (Dublin: Dominicana Publications, 1994). *First
Prologue*, p. 4.

However, these local administrative areas were by then unusually small, thanks to the 1348 plague which is estimated to have reduced the population of the city by as much as 80 per cent.[9]

The small groupings that emerge from Tuscan political history have a part to play in Catherine's story. Not only did she know everyone around her: she was known by everyone in her community, and her fame would pass quickly from one community to the next. Similarly, political leaders were known to, and rooted in, their community. Access to them was easy and routine, and Catherine had no difficulty in making her views known to people in power. And without the divisions and hostilities that the preference for small groups engendered, Catherine would have been deprived of a significant part of her peace-making activities.

Passing pilgrims

A further cause of Siena's prosperity was the result not of wars and conquests but of simple piety—the ever-increasing popularity of pilgrimage and the economic benefits that it offered to stopping places along the way. Siena was situated on the Via Francigena (also known as the Via Romea), the main route to Rome for those pilgrims journeying from northern Europe. Indeed, the road was favoured not because of its quality but because of the number of stopping places it offered, where pilgrims would stay for days or even weeks. Places like Siena also had a thriving souvenir industry, and pilgrims would take home with them small items as proof of where they had been. An early visitor of note was the Archbishop of Canterbury in 990. Archbishop Sigeric, known as "the Serious", spent a few days in Siena on his way back from Rome (where he had received his "pallium" or mantle of investiture from the pope) to Canterbury.

For Catherine growing up in Siena, the sight of groups of foreign pilgrims was a common one. And they brought with them stories of the wider world, stories of saints and sinners that they had picked up on their

---

[9]   Malcolm Barber notes that around 1300 the city contained around 50,000 people, with a further 62,000 living in the country area within a thirty-mile radius: see *The Two Cities: Medieval Europe 1050–1320* (Abingdon: Routledge, 1992), p. 270.

travels. For girls like Catherine, these pilgrims also offered entirely new role models: independent women travelling on their own, experiencing new places and new customs, but guided above all by an elevated and holy purpose.

Catherine's childhood

In their own secret place, in the home of their ringleader, a group of little girls are playing "let's pretend". In this timeless game, children imitate the adults whom they see as the role models of their day—parents, doctors, teachers or shopkeepers. This particular group base their play on what they know best: the rituals of the church that they all attend without question and that dominates the lives of their parents.

The toys that some of the children from richer families play with are dolls representing Mary or the infant Jesus. The wall paintings and rudimentary statues in the church have fired their imaginations as, with the help of their dolls, they act out scenes from the Bible or from Tuscan church history. This particular group pretend they are monks or nuns, priests or bishops, or the mysterious ones known simply as the holy people.

Their leader, a bossy child, acts out the part of a holy woman. She preaches to her flock, admonishing them for their misdeeds. She is well organized, drawing up endless plans for their salvation, setting out the number of Our Fathers and Hail Marys that her friends must say by way of atonement. And the others demand to have their turn as preacher and confessor. But there is a darker side to their game. Their leader is passionate in declaring her own sinfulness as well as theirs. She takes sticks and fallen branches to beat herself on the back as best she can. And her playmates follow suit, acting out in their own way the dramas that they have seen pictured in the church, in the lives of saints and martyrs.

This is Catherine as a six-year-old, as Raymond portrays her, drawing her friends into a frame which very soon for her will be not so much play acting as a way of life. Does she take her friends to a secret place because that is what children do? Or because she senses adult disapproval? Raymond's passing reference to Catherine at play is there to offer a glimpse of what is to come: Catherine the holy woman, the founder of a women's monastery, a dedicated ascetic, and a leader to be reckoned with.[10] Yet, unlike previous biographies, his writing is sufficiently evocative to allow his readers to create their own mental picture of holiness in the making.

While, for example, Clare of Montefalco's biographer, in referring to her childhood, observed only his subject's deep commitment to obedience from the age of six, Raymond gives more detail about Catherine, attributing his information mainly to her mother, Lapa.[11] Like Lombardelli's biographies, but at much greater length, Raymond's has a full chapter on birth and infancy; this includes several visions, an incidence of levitation and a reference to Catherine's growing aversion to food. At one point, Raymond hints at a similarity with the infancy of Jesus: "The little one grew and waxed strong, in readiness for the day when she would be filled with the Holy Spirit and the wisdom of God" (cf. Luke 2:52).[12] And offering a strong hint as to Catherine's future path he writes:

> ... in those hidden years ... by a knowledge infused in her by the Holy Spirit, she learned and took to heart the virtues and the way of life of the ancient Egyptian Fathers of the desert and the life-stories of some of the saints, especially of Saint Dominic.[13]

This emphasis on the work of the Holy Spirit both distances Catherine from the accounts of the holy women before her (where reference to the Spirit is often singularly lacking) and establishes from the outset that her life will be something special.

---

[10]   *Life of Catherine of Siena*, pp. 31-2.

[11]   By contrast, this is Raymond's only comment on the childhood of Agnes of Montepulciano, at least before she felt a clear calling to religious life around the age of nine: "Sprouting in childhood that devotion which ought to germinate abundantly in adulthood, she dismissed her little playmates, neglected childish games, and withdrew to a secret place at the back of the house by the wall. There, as she devoutly learned, with bended knees and folded hands, she still more devoutly played" (*Life of St Agnes of Montepulciano*, pp. 7-8).

[12]   *Life of Catherine of Siena*, p. 28.

[13]   Ibid., p. 30.

A saint at home

Raymond of Capua's access to Catherine's family and her mother in particular enables him to establish a fresh picture of holiness: that of the saint at home. We know relatively little about the domestic circumstances of the holy women who preceded Catherine. For them, home was a place to leave—either to escape (Umiltà of Faenza) or to move to a religious community funded by a wealthy father (Clare of Montefalco). Or, in the case of older women, they had no home, as was the plight of Margaret of Cortona after the death of her lover.

For Catherine, the model appears at first sight to be different. Her home as a child was the place of her early piety; yet Raymond presents it too as a place of conflict and restraint.[14] Like some other holy women, in particular Lombardelli's somewhat stereotyped visionaries, Catherine's vow of virginity soon clashed with her family's marriage plans for her. Raymond notes that it was the custom of the country for girls to be kept at home once they had reached puberty, while a suitable husband was sought for them. So for Catherine her safe place, where her knowledge and love of God could deepen and grow, became almost overnight a place of confinement and danger. In a growing rift with her parents, Catherine at first rejected her mother's demands that she should wear make-up and take care of her hair and complexion, whereupon Lapa solicited the help of Catherine's married sister Buonaventura, to whom she was particularly close. Despite agreeing to make herself attractive, Catherine was not to be swayed from her resolve not to marry. Even so, this episode was sufficient to distract her—"the fervour of her prayer cooled off", says Raymond[15]—and her bond with her sister, who subsequently died in childbirth, was broken. At a stroke, domestic harmony was replaced with conflict and tragedy, with the unfortunate Buonaventura, who had

---

[14]   In this, Raymond is following what Palmer observes of the lives of saints of a much earlier age: "The breaking up of blood families and the creation of spiritual ones became something of a monastic and hagiographical trope", James T. Palmer, *Early Medieval Hagiography* (Ashland, OH: Arc Humanities Press, 2018), p. 93.

[15]   *Life of Catherine of Siena*, p. 43.

failed to appreciate Catherine's calling, being dismissed as "enticing her on the path of vanity".[16]

In the lives of holy women, family conflicts centring on finding a husband for a reluctant daughter are nothing new. As Luongo puts it, they were "practically a hagiographical requirement for a saintly virgin".[17] So Catherine's home becomes the place for serious evil, as "the old Enemy" stirs up her relatives to force Catherine into marriage. Her previously loving and apparently pious parents now try to break her, first by enlisting the help of an unnamed Dominican (who encourages Catherine to cut off her hair—as did Katherine of Alexandria—to reduce her physical attractiveness) and, when this fails, forcing her to work in the kitchen, without any time or private space for prayer.[18]

There is no outsider in the form of a handsome prince to enter this Cinderella-like story and deliver the young woman from this domestic cruelty. Rather, it is the Holy Spirit who inspires Catherine to replace her lost place of meditation by "a secret cell within her own heart". And as the abuse continues, she is inspired to imagine she is serving Christ, his mother and the apostles instead of her own family: "Picturing them in this fashion she was able to render them a cheerful and unfailing service which filled them with astonishment."[19] So Catherine is depicted as having a spiritual home within a predominantly hostile physical home, all the time that her family's opposition to her being received into the Dominican Order persists. Once she has taken the Dominican habit

---

[16]   Ibid., p. 44.

[17]   N. 2 above, p. 28.

[18]   Raymond reports that when Catherine was deprived of her own bedroom, she chose to share a room with her brother Stefano. Because he was at work all day, she was able to pray there privately, but on condition that the door was left open. This lack of privacy was turned to good effect when her father Giacomo—described by Raymond as "more God-fearing than the rest" (p. 52)—witnessed a white dove above his daughter while she was at prayer and declared that Catherine must now be free to take her vows as she wished. According to Raymond, however, Catherine's relationship with her mother remained difficult.

[19]   *Life of Catherine of Siena*, p. 48.

Catherine will continue to live at home, but she will have her own room and will be free to come and go as she pleases. Thus, in exploring the ancient hagiographic convention of family opposition, Raymond adapts and embellishes it in order to create a new perspective on his subject's early life and to present it as a significant stage in her developing holiness.

Catherine the Dominican

"There is no difference in the sight of God between men and women in the performance of the works of salvation."[20]

The Benincasa home lay barely a stone's throw from the great church of S. Domenico, which dates from 1226, and whose fourteenth-century bell tower (campanile) was constructed just a few years before Catherine was born. For this reason alone, she would have been unlikely to have been attracted to any other Order, and Raymond describes her as a child being captivated by the sight of Dominicans going about their business locally. It was in one of the chapels of S. Domenico that Catherine received her habit, and where today her portrait by Andrea Vanni is housed. The cappella di Santa Caterina was specially built around the time of Catherine's canonization to accommodate a reliquary containing her head.

From the outset the Dominicans were clearly different from the other Orders, with their specific call to pursue an apostolic life of itinerant preaching, designed in the first instance to take on heretical preachers on their own ground. Preaching, and by implication associated intellectual activities, was what they were about. The same was not true for their female adherents, at least initially, whose role was limited to praying for the work of the Friars. The Order of Dominican nuns was established because of the demand for a well-regulated religious life, but, as Simon Tugwell points out, "Some of the monasteries of Dominican nuns were not initially inspired by any specifically Dominican vision, and it is sometimes difficult to see what difference it really made to them that they

---

[20] New Statutes of the Congregation of Our Lady, Arezzo (1262), in Simon Tugwell (ed.), *Early Dominicans: Selected Writings* (London: SPCK, 1982), p. 444.

were Dominicans."[21] Nonetheless, as far as Catherine was concerned, apart from their physical proximity, the Dominican emphasis on combating heresy would be more than enough to direct her activities in the future.

Raymond does not specify Catherine's age when she experienced a vision in which Dominic and "founders of the various religious orders" all appeared to her, with Dominic holding out to her a habit of the Sisters of Penance.[22] With her resolve thus stiffened, Catherine is able to overcome the continuing opposition of her mother in particular, which is presumably set out in order to illustrate a satanic reaction to this turning point in her life.

When Catherine Benincasa first requested admission to the Sisters of Penance of St Dominic, she was refused: it was reserved for widows "of matured age and unblemished reputation who desired to dedicate themselves to the service of God". The Sisters lived in their own homes and were subject to a discipline which it was felt a young girl could not attain. Catherine fell ill and at her mother's urgent request the Sisters agreed to visit her and assess her potential. Their chief concern was her looks: if she was too attractive her request would be denied for fear of scandal. Raymond comments with brutal honesty that "even under normal circumstances [Catherine] had nothing out of the ordinary in the way of good looks",[23] and in any case her illness had temporarily marred her appearance. With the agreement of all the Sisters and the Friars who looked after them, Catherine was allowed to take the habit. This meant, of course, that she was the first virgin to do so, setting her apart in her chosen Order and in her city from the very beginning. Raymond comments:

> In view of this I make bold to say that the habit never reached its full and due perfection in Siena until this virgin put it on and wore it. She was the first and the best in her city to receive the habit as a virgin; since her time many other virgins there have followed in her footsteps, so that the words of David can be applied to her: "In her train shall virgins be brought to the King".[24]

[21]   Tugwell, *Early Dominicans*, p. 29.

[22]   *Life of Catherine of* Siena, p. 50.

[23]   Ibid., p. 66.

[24]   Ibid., p. 68.

The Dominican habit—black for humility, white for innocence—now took on a new meaning. In Raymond's portrayal of Catherine, the white will symbolize virginal purity,[25] which the artists will reinforce by including the traditional iconography of a lily indicating virginity. In other words, Raymond does not hesitate to tweak traditional symbolism in order to promote both the saint and her city.[26]

According to Simon Tugwell, the Sisters had "a social rather than a doctrinal apostolate",[27] running hospitals and organizing help for the poor. Catherine would certainly do her share of that, but even in the fourteenth century she had a "doctrinal apostolate" that was exceptional for her time. Her choice to follow Dominic took her into a setting of learning and of involvement in the world, which would define her ministry in the years ahead.

Taking control: Fasting, penitence and isolation

Voluntary starvation, charitable food distribution and Eucharistic devotion were all means by which women controlled their social and religious circumstances quite directly and effectively.[28]

---

[25] Raymond argues that Catherine's "virginal innocence . . . ranks higher than any chastity of widowhood". Ibid.

[26] It is possible that Raymond is also tweaking Dominican history in order to establish Catherine as their foremost female saint. Luongo argues (above, p. 37, n. 2) that the Dominican Third Order, the Order of Penance, was not in existence around 1370, and sees this episode as symptomatic of a lack of distinction between "regular" and "irregular" or cloistered/uncloistered religious women. If Raymond is indeed bringing forward the date of the Third Order's foundation, it would be because he clearly would not want Catherine to be seen as anything other than fully regular in her admission to the Order.

[27] Tugwell, pp. 29, 30.

[28] Caroline Walker Bynum, *Holy Feast and Holy Fast: The Religious Significance of Food to Medieval Women* (Berkeley: University of California Press, 1992), p. 220.

Caroline Walker Bynum argues persuasively that women's food practices in general, and not just eating disorders in particular, enabled women to control those around them from puberty onwards, as well as to exercise rigid control of themselves. While the later Italian holy women inherited a strict ascetic tradition from their immediate predecessors and ultimately from the practices of the earliest Christian saints, some aspects of these controlling food practices were peculiar to the time.

Giving away food to the poor, for example, although on the face of it a laudable practice (and one that Catherine shared with Umiltà), Walker Bynum sees as a way of rejecting the values of lower- or middle-class parents who were proud of their achievement in feeding their families and the social status that carried with it. More generally, refusing to eat is, among other things, an effective way of distancing oneself from the family gathered together at mealtimes and from the economic status their food represents. Coupled with other practices that conflicted with normal family life, the effect could be devastating. Walker Bynum comments:

> By a series of ascetic behaviors, Catherine slowly forged for herself, without ever leaving home, a life whose values were utterly different from those of her wealthy merchant father and her doting, efficient mother with a brood of twenty children.[29]

Although Raymond interrupts his story of Catherine rejecting marriage to reflect on the future saint's lifelong asceticism,[30] there is no indication that at the time when she rejected any concession to physical attraction by cutting off her hair she was also trying to change her appearance by near-starvation. Catherine's extreme abstinence from food and drink is only highlighted when Raymond considers the period between the end of her family's opposition and the start of her life as a Dominican, that is, when she once again has her own small room where "she began to live in it as in the desert, herself alone with God alone, and to mortify her body to her heart's content".[31] And even then, Raymond has little to

---

[29]   Ibid., p. 224.

[30]   *Life of Catherine of Siena*, p. 43.

[31]   Ibid., p. 54.

say (and maybe knew very little as well) on matters of detail. We are told that Catherine had rarely eaten meat and gradually gave up wine and cooked food, eventually, by the age of about twenty, restricting herself to water and uncooked vegetables. Catherine, we learn, also slept on wooden planks and forced herself to go without sleep. Three times a day she would scourge herself with an iron chain, following the example of St Dominic.

All this, even in the privacy of a virtual cell, causes considerable distress to Catherine's mother, who would describe to Raymond how her formerly "able-bodied and robust" daughter had wasted away. This is a further opportunity for the biographer to note satanic intervention, as the "Ancient Serpent" "made use of [Lapa's] too human maternal love which put concern for her daughter's body above concern for her soul"[32] and encouraged her to try to end her daughter's penitential practices.

In her home within a home, Catherine succeeds in establishing a way of life that is diametrically opposed to the lives of those in the home around her. In the figure of Lapa, with her very basic maternal instincts, the two homes are brought together in a jarringly uncomfortable way. The clash between mother and daughter, which in Raymond's account sometimes even borders on the comical,[33] is symbolized above all in the portrayal of an anorexic young woman in whom, Raymond goes so far as to claim, the rejection of food is nothing less than a spiritual gift, "a unique chrism".[34] In imitating the example of holy women and men who have gone before her, Catherine succeeds in creating a persona that is both physically and spiritually apart from those around her, and in the process causes them extreme discomfort—a discomfort that is increasingly evident in the work of Raymond her biographer and confessor.

Indeed, Raymond's attempt to portray Catherine's family, in particular her mother and sister, as the wicked agents of temptation, could be said to backfire. Their evident love and concern for Catherine leads them

---

[32]   Ibid., p. 61.

[33]   When Catherine fails to trick her mother into believing that she had abandoned her mortification of the flesh, Lapa exclaims, "It's useless for me to be bothering my head ... you are set on having your own way. I may as well close my eyes to what is going on." Ibid., p. 62.

[34]   Ibid.

to behave as most families would, first offering her a possible (and face-saving) way out from what might have been a misguided sense of vocation, and, second, attempting to persuade her to moderate her excessive practices for the sake of her health—and they would certainly not be alone in that. Raymond depicts Catherine's rejection of these efforts as evidence of her conviction that the traditional ways of the mystics were incompatible with normal life. Even the provision of Catherine's own small space does not allow her any real escape from contact with the world around her, even in its most benign form. In her struggles to bring ancient practices of holiness into the family home, Catherine's story highlights above all the new challenges that this way of life, fostered by the discipline of the penitential Third Orders, inevitably presents, both for the penitent herself and for those around her.

The family's turmoil does not end with Catherine's reception of her Dominican habit. Raymond tells us that while this does not require her to take vows of chastity, obedience and poverty, Catherine nonetheless adopts this way of life for herself. This creates the final clash with her father's wealthy household with whom she shared a roof. Unable to bear the sight of comfortable living at such close quarters, Catherine prays that the family's worldly goods should be taken away, so that they might not experience the temptations represented by wealth. And in due course the family was reduced to total poverty. Catherine's "high regard for poverty"[35] leads her in the end to bring down those closest to her, as her inner world triumphs over the home in which it is set.

Later in life Catherine seems to recognize the damage done to her by the eating habits formed in her teenage years, but the time for change is long past. In a letter addressed to "A religious man in Florence who was shocked at her ascetic practices", she reveals her predicament and her apparent despair at being unable to escape it:

> I have always forced myself once or twice a day to take food. And I have prayed constantly, and do pray God, and shall pray Him that in this matter of eating He will give me grace to live like other creatures, if it is His will—for it is mine. I tell you . . . I

---

[35]   Ibid., p. 75.

enter within myself, to recognize my infirmity, and God . . . has made me correct the sin of gluttony.[36]

She ends with a rather sad plea: "I beg you that if you see any remedy you will write of it; and provided it be for the honour of God, I will accept it willingly."

By then, however, Catherine's starvation practices had become an intrinsic part of her spiritual life. Like other holy women, she finds it sufficient to receive the Sacrament in order to feel "complete nourishment", but she takes this a step further by claiming that:

> . . . the very presence and sight of it upon the altar is food to me . . . the very presence of a priest, when I know that he has touched the Blessed Sacrament, is such a source of strength to me that all thought of other food is banished.[37]

Unlike most of her predecessors, however, Catherine's visions provide her with an extreme source of food: not only the sacramental realization of the body and blood of Christ but the person of Jesus himself. In her ecstatic devotion to the body of the wounded Saviour, Catherine is permitted not only to touch his wounds but to drink the blood from his pierced side—in Raymond's words "drinking from the fountain of Life".[38] While this may seem an unappealing blessing, at least to twenty-first

---

[36]   Vida D. Scudder (tr. and ed.), *Saint Catherine of Siena as seen in her letters*, p. 38, available at <https://www.gutenberg.org/ebooks/7403>, accessed 24 September 2021. Gluttony in others, which she equates with enjoyment of food, was equally abhorrent to Catherine. In a letter to Ristoro Canigiani, the brother of one of her secretaries, she writes: "Avoid being at intemperate banquets, but live moderately, like a man who does not want to make a god of his belly. But take food for need, and not for the wretched pleasure it gives. For it is impossible that any man who does not govern himself in eating should keep himself innocent." Ibid., p. 90.

[37]   *Life of Catherine of Siena*, p. 165.

[38]   Ibid., p. 173. Aldobrandesca had a similar experience. See her *Vita*, Chapter 21, "Come le fu concesso gustare del Sangue uscito del Costato del Crocifisso".

century Protestants, it represents a logical progression from drinking the blood of Christ in the Eucharist. It is, though, a privilege that is reserved for a very few. This action, repeated in several of Catherine's visions, is taken as an explanation of her ability to survive without food and at the same time it enables her to receive "those graces of the spirit which were showered upon her in such profusion".[39] In short, bodily food and spiritual food have become totally incompatible.

The Black Death

It is strange that Raymond makes no mention of the plague that struck Siena just a year after Catherine was born. Since her mother was the main source of Raymond's information, that would surely have been something a mother would not forget, given the danger it would have posed to her young family, including, now, the last child, Giovanna. Writing of the effects of the plague in England, Nicholas Orme notes that while many children would have died in 1348–49, the impact of a second wave in 1360–62 was felt on the young across Europe, and it appears that children were particularly badly hit by this and other epidemics of the time.[40]

Indeed, successive waves of plague and its economic effects form an ongoing backdrop to Catherine's life. In 1374, according to Vida D. Scudder, the Benincasa household was directly affected, as Lapa was bringing up eleven grandchildren in her own house, eight of whom died, and there is a suggestion that Catherine herself buried them.[41]

Wickham estimates that by the end of the century, the population in Europe was half what it had been in 1346, when the Black Death was first noted (in Crimea). In his view, though, this was not all bad news. With the workforce halved, there was more land available to peasant farmers,

---

[39]   Ibid.

[40]   Nicholas Orme, *Medieval Children* (New Haven: Yale University Press, 2001), p. 107.

[41]   Scudder, *Saint Catherine of Siena as seen in her letters*, p. 27.

and there were more jobs for workers moving from the countryside into towns and cities, with prosperity increasing accordingly.[42]

Alice Curtayne, however, highlights the plague's adverse effects on the Church, which she considers never fully recovered its former number of clergy. In order to survive, religious communities had to cut short their selection and training procedures, and young, uneducated clergy were ordained in order to maintain public worship.[43] If this was indeed the case, Catherine's dedication to building up the Church would have an important part to play.

A further outbreak of plague in Siena in or around 1373 gives Raymond the opportunity to focus on Catherine's many miracles of healing at this time, not least because he himself also fell ill and was cured by her. Raymond had been visiting the sick "in consequence of that zeal for souls which is native to my Order since its foundation",[44] when he contracted the plague and was saved when apparently close to death thanks to the prayers of Catherine who was "rapt out of her senses".[45] Other Dominicans were also cured, and Raymond extends his account of plague victims to include Catherine's healing miracles on other occasions, especially where the good and the great are in attendance.

So, for example, when Catherine returned home ahead of Gregory XI on his journey from Avignon to Rome, there is a veritable travelogue of healing miracles, including a sick child at Toulon, and one of her secretaries, described as a "good religious man", while they are staying at Genoa. Later, when Gregory sends Catherine to Florence with a mandate to bring peace with the Florentines, a Dominican sister in her party is also cured of a swollen foot.[46] Given the hazards of fourteenth-century travel, of course, it is no surprise that Catherine on her travels should have had many such opportunities. However, since Raymond was himself

---

[42] Chris Wickham, *Medieval Europe* (New Haven: Yale University Press, 2016), pp. 210–11, 214.

[43] Alice Curtayne, *Saint Catherine of Siena* (London: Sheed & Ward, 1929, reissued by Tan Books and Publishers Inc., 1980), p. xiii.

[44] *Life of Catherine of Siena*, p. 232.

[45] Ibid., p. 240.

[46] Ibid., p. 248.

immersed in ministry to the sick, his concern to promote the role of the Dominican Order in this regard is equally unsurprising. And by anchoring some of Catherine's miracles in a time of plague he ensures that her (and their) compassion and disregard for personal safety will be remembered.

The Example of St Francis

In 1224 St Francis of Assisi underwent a forty-day fast on Mount La Verna in the Tuscan Apennines, around seventy miles north of Assisi, which is today a place of pilgrimage. There he received physical marks on his body, corresponding to the five wounds of Christ on the cross, from a seraph who appeared to him in the form of a crucified man, himself bearing the same wounds. According to his biographer, Francis suffered bleeding from his hands, feet and sides, until his death two years later. And while Francis is the first and probably the best-known of medieval stigmatics, thanks not least to the importance of his Order and the artists who portrayed him, stigmatization was subsequently experienced in various forms by lesser figures, lay and ordained, men and women alike.

Intense devotion to Christ's Passion and the Eucharist was undoubtedly a contributory factor in the spread of this experience, particularly among women. Subsequent devotions, such as that of the wound in the side (that led to the cult of the Sacred Heart) and of the Five Sacred Wounds, also had a part to play. In its most common form, stigmatization was said to be invisible, meaning that people felt pain in their hands and feet or on their foreheads (a wound from Christ's crown of thorns) but without exhibiting any external signs, an experience common to Clare of Montefalco and later Catherine of Genoa.

The experience of Catherine in receiving invisible stigmata had far-reaching consequences, and not just because of her gender. Perhaps predictably, the long-standing tensions between Franciscans and Dominicans meant that the latter seized on the opportunity to have their own holy woman enjoying the same spiritual status as Francis. And the recognition of Catherine's stigmatization fluctuated according to the sympathies of the pope at the time. The writer Gregorio Lombardelli was eventually given the task by Pope Clement VIII of defending Catherine's case, in his *Sommario della disputa a difesa delle sacre stimate di Santa Caterina da Siena* (Summary of the dispute in defence of the sacred stigmata of St Catherine of Siena) published in 1601, although it would be another thirty years before Urban VIII officially recognized her as a stigmatic saint, long after her canonization (in 1461). Interestingly, on this occasion, Catherine's city had a part to play. Carolyn Muessig notes:

> The agreement had been finalized by the hard work of the Sienese who sent one of their local gentlemen, Lorenzo Petrucci, to represent their cause in Rome in 1629. Lorenzo preserved the details of his trip and negotiations with Vatican officials in a journal recording his sojourn to Rome where he argued diplomatically and tirelessly for Catherine to be recognized as bearer of the five wounds of Christ.[47]

It is, however, with Catherine and her invisible stigmata that the work of artists takes centre stage in conveying an understanding of her as a stigmatic. Obviously unable to depict something that was not present, they chose instead to imitate the model of St Francis and show her as visibly bearing the wounds of Christ in her body. This led to an unusual intervention by Church authorities as successive popes first banned and then permitted images depicting Catherine with visible wounds (for examples, see Chapter 7 below).

---

[47]   Carolyn Muessig, *The Stigmata in Medieval and Early Modern Europe* (Oxford: Oxford University Press, 2020), p. 186.

Conclusion: Catherine in her own words

Given the sheer volume of material devoted to "Catherine studies", it is unnecessary to attempt any additional critical assessment of her writings.[48] However, by way of conclusion, a few pointers may be helpful in establishing the contrast between Catherine and her Tuscan predecessors.

Although Catherine could read Latin, she was unable to write it and as a consequence her substantial body of work was dictated. Unlike previous holy women, and perhaps because of her ever-growing reputation, she had a small army of secretaries to draw on, so there is no single scribe particularly associated with her. In addition, the *Dialogue* was dictated while she was in ecstasy, resulting in occasional obscurities in meaning. Nonetheless, by any standards this is a masterpiece, with the circumstances of its dictation simply adding a new dimension to her work, which is essentially a genre of ecstatic writing.

While Umiltà's *Sermoni* also contained ecstatic dialogues with divine figures, there was little sense of losing touch with the human person who reveals them, and with her didactic purpose. Catherine's dialogue with God, however, is more intensely visionary, and demands a new mindset from the reader. A good example are the sixty-two chapters of the *Dialogo* that Cavallini groups under the heading of "The Bridge". Their main subject relates to the three steps of the soul on a journey from imperfection to perfection, and union with God. Although many mystics enumerated the steps they believed were needed to attain perfection, three is unusually low (and here perfection is in fact achieved after only two), in contrast to, at the other extreme, Angela of Foligno's proposed thirty steps.

Catherine uses the image of Christ as the "Bridge" between earth and heaven. The Bridge passes over a river of tempestuous waters, saving the soul from drowning in the world's sin. In attaining the first step, the soul climbs up out of the river and is thereby stripped of vice, with the second

---

48   The critical editions of the Letters, Prayers and the *Dialogue* by Suzanne Noffke are particularly recommended as well as other books and articles by the same author, who is herself a Dominican.

it is filled with love and virtue, while with the third it tastes peace. The first step is represented by the pierced feet of Christ, echoed in the efforts of the "feet" of the soul. The second step is Christ's heart, which reveals the secrets of his head (his love), and this is already the state of perfection. The third step is Christ's mouth that speaks the word of truth.

The metaphor fluctuates and shifts its frame of reference, which makes visualization of what is being described a little challenging. The efforts to climb *out of* the water by those described as "imperfect" climbers because they are motivated by "servile fear" are also portrayed as a boat out of control *on* the water:

> There are many who begin their climb so sluggishly and pay what they owe me in such bits and pieces, so indifferently and ignorantly, that they quickly fall by the way. The smallest wind makes them hoist their sails and turn back. They had climbed only imperfectly to the first stair of Christ crucified, and so they never reach the second, which is that of his heart.[49]

The soul must therefore serve God not out of fear but out of love, and it is a love which must not be for the servants' own profit or revealed in imperfect love for their neighbour.

The onus here lies on the reader to receive Catherine's ecstatic words in a state of mind that is as close to hers as is possible, and to allow oneself to be inspired by it. Any expectation of a blow-by-blow account of human behaviour is bound to be disappointed.

The tone of Catherine's letters, on the other hand, is vivid and down to earth, whether offering practical advice to her fellow religious or rebuking the powerful in the world. There are also collections of her prayers, many of which occur spontaneously in the course of her other writings, and these offer the most accessible insight into her theology and spirituality, in which devotion to the Trinity and the guidance and inspiration of the Holy Spirit are all-important. Some of these prayers are contemplative, but others are straightforward intercessions, such as prayers for the pope,

---

[49] *Dialogue*, n. 3 above, p. 113.

for the renewal of the Church, for the Church's priests and for her own confessors.

Whereas the voices of Angela and Umiltà remain largely unheard outside their Order and their immediate surroundings, Catherine's *Dialogue*, although written down in Latin, is an important contribution to the history of literature in the Italian peninsula. The simple passage of time, with a rapidly changing cultural scene and ever-increasing literacy, is one obvious explanation for this, as is the prestigious setting of fourteenth-century Siena itself. What cannot be ruled out, however, is the underlying yet persistent influence of Catherine's predecessors. Holy women are no longer the "problem" outsiders that they once were—so much so that both Catherine of Siena and Bridget of Sweden are able to emerge as respected national figures.

Thanks not least, then, to the women from the Tuscan hills who went before her, Catherine's short life, combining national activity, intellectual agility and powerful spiritual insight, has rightly remained an inspiration to the Church down the centuries. The cementing of Catherine's reputation by her biographer and artists will be the subject of Chapter 7.

CHAPTER 6

Engaging with popes and princes

"I have the joy of proclaiming *three new co-patronesses of the European continent.* They are: St Edith Stein, St Bridget of Sweden and St Catherine of Siena.

"[They] are all linked in a special way with the continent's history. Edith Stein . . . is the symbol of Europe's tragedies in this century. Bridget of Sweden and Catherine of Siena, who both lived in the fourteenth century, worked tirelessly for the Church, taking her fortunes to heart on a European scale."

Pope John Paul II, Homily to the Second Special Assembly for Europe of the Synod of Bishops, 1 October 1999.

Europe already had three patron saints—Benedict, Cyril and Methodius— and in creating three "co-patronesses" to set alongside them, Pope John Paul was probably seeking to deflect criticism of his policy of excluding women from ministry in the Church. He took the opportunity to assert the Church's lasting recognition of what he called "the full spiritual dignity of women", from Mary the Mother of Jesus onwards, and claimed that they have been honoured "with no less fervour" than holy men. It may be questioned whether Catherine's intentions were genuinely European in the sense we understand that today. Her primary concern was unity in the Church under a pope in Rome, and her travels were confined to a relatively small area in Italy and France. To claim, as Pope John Paul went on to do in his homily, that Catherine "brought peace to her native Siena, Italy and fourteenth-century Europe" is a little exaggerated, however much she may have longed for that peace.

Raymond begins the second part of his life of Catherine with a description of Christ's call to Catherine to begin to move among "people in the world" (probably around 1370), and this is the setting for the remainder of his narrative. Almost his entire focus in this worldly aspect of Catherine's ministry, though, is on Catherine's "charity", and in particular the miracles that she performed for the poor and the sick alongside her. Raymond refers in passing to various journeys he undertook with Catherine, but again really only to highlight the miracles she performed along the way. Episodes that are well attested elsewhere but which might have attracted charges of scandal are simply not mentioned. It would appear from Raymond's book that "the world" is simply a new arena in which Catherine could exercise her gifts and continue her ecstatic practices. This continues to be the case with miracles performed after Catherine's death. Raymond notes how Roman forces defeated an army sent from Naples to try to capture the pope. Nonetheless, a number of Romans were taken prisoner, but "all . . . who called at once upon Catherine were miraculously freed from their chains, with no hand helping them but that of God, and made their way safe and sound to Rome."[1]

Indeed, it is probably unrealistic to try to separate the Church and the world in an era where the two are politically inseparable. Gerald Parsons comments that those promoting Catherine as a patron saint all appeal to the "politically motivated Catherine" of the last six or seven years of her life,[2] but the politics that motivated her were those of the inextricably linked Church and state, at a time when sanctity and worldly affairs were fully compatible.[3] Furthermore, Catherine had a model for her activities in the person of another "co-patroness of Europe", Bridget (Birgitta) of Sweden.

---

[1]   *Life of Catherine of Siena*, p. 359.

[2]   Gerald Parsons, *The Cult of Saint Catherine of Siena: A Study in Civil Religion* (Farnham: Ashgate, 2008), p. 160.

[3]   As noted by F. Thomas Luongo in his conclusion to *The Saintly Politics of Catherine of Siena* (New York: Cornell University Press, 2006), p. 206.

The example of St Bridget of Sweden

Although Catherine and Bridget were near contemporaries, and despite the fact that Bridget lived in Rome from 1350 until her death in 1373, it appears that the two women never met, although there must have been some contact between Catherine and Bridget's daughter, also called Catherine.[4] Yet it seems unlikely that Catherine was not inspired by the Scandinavian saint, at least in respect of Bridget's fearless challenge of the status quo, and their shared concern about the danger of schism and the integrity of the Church and Church leaders.

In Bridget, Catherine had the example of a woman whose primary vocation was to be prophetic. This does not rule out mystical experience as well. As McGinn puts it, "[Bridget] certainly enjoyed an easy familiarity with God and the heavenly world . . . [but her] primary identity was more that of a channel of heavenly calls for reforming the church in a time of crisis."[5]

The tone of Bridget's criticisms is considerably more strident than anything we hear from Catherine. Bridget had a reputation for being "difficult", and her description of convents as being "more like brothels than holy cloisters"[6] would not have endeared her to her fellow religious, while her attack on an unnamed bishop is merciless, comparing him to a monkey.[7] Her general condemnation

---

[4]   Raymond reports that Pope Urban VI devised a plan to send the two Catherines to Naples to dissuade Queen Giovanna from supporting the schismatics, a scheme that was firmly rejected by the Swedish Catherine, whereupon it fell to Raymond to convince the pope that it was not a good idea to put the women's safety and reputation at risk. *Life of Catherine of Siena*, pp. 311–12.

[5]   Bernard McGinn, *The Varieties of Vernacular Mysticism 1350–1550* (New York: Crossroad Publishing Co., 2012), pp. 192–3.

[6]   Darrell Wright (ed.), *The Revelations of Saint Bridget of Sweden (1303–1373): Books 1–5* (ebook 2016), Book 4, Chapter 33.

[7]   Ibid., Book 3, Chapter 11.

of the clergy is that they have failed to live up to their calling to "proclaim [God's] words and to demonstrate it in [their] actions". The words that she is given by God are that the archetypical cleric "has become leprous and mute. Anyone who looks to see a fine and virtuous character in him shrinks back at the sight and shudders to approach him because of the leprosy of his pride and greed."[8]

As for the laity, Bridget particularly directs her fury at the people of Rome, who are guilty, among much else, of sacrilegious behaviour, the misuse of indulgences and a failure to receive Holy Communion regularly. She does, however, put in a special plea for those, both lay and ordained, who "have been like orphans due to the pope's absence, but . . . have defended the see of their father like sons and have wisely opposed the traitors, persevering in the midst of such hardship".[9]

Immoderate language is also characteristic of the revelations given to Bridget about Pope Gregory. It is presented as God's clear will that the pope should return to Rome, and despite his many failings (including favouring the rich with the goods of the poor) Gregory is promised that "the sooner you come to Rome, the sooner you will experience an increase of virtue and of the gifts of the Holy Spirit and the more you will be inflamed with the divine fire of my love. Come, then, and do not delay!"[10]

Bridget addresses the warring kings of France and England in a revelation that she receives from the Virgin Mary, who intercedes with her Son on their behalf. In a long and colourful description, the two kingdoms are presented as "two most ferocious beasts" with a "horrible roar" and their kings are "full of the fire of anger and greed". The Son's response is that redemption is possible: the kings are "outside the door" on which they must knock, but it will be opened to those who pray.[11]

---

8   Ibid., Book 2, Chapter 20.

9   Ibid., Book 4, Chapter 33.

10   Ibid., Book 4, Chapter 142.

11   Ibid., Book 4, Chapter 104.

Catherine and the Church

> You will give proofs of the Spirit that is in you, before small and
> great, before layfolk and clergy and religious, for I will give you
> a mouth and a wisdom which none shall be able to resist. I will
> bring you before Pontiffs and Rulers of Churches and of the
> Christian people, in order that I may do as is my way, and use
> what is weak to put to shame the pride of the strong.[12]

This is Catherine's great commission, that she received from her "Eternal
Spouse" in an ecstatic vision. Her mission is first and foremost to the
Church rather than to princes and powers, although in the 1370s the two
were not always easily separable. When she addressed worldly rulers, it
was always in the interests of the Church, and above all the papacy.

Catherine never questioned the validity or the integrity of the papacy.
For her, the pope was, quite simply, God's representative on earth and
the head of the Church. She was utterly loyal to the popes of her day
and addressed them with deep respect, although this did not prevent
her from reproaching them for, on occasions, what she perceived as
their weakness or timidity. In turn, the papacy had a defining role in
Catherine's ministry as she worked tirelessly to end conflict and restore
unity within the Church she loved. After her death a number of popes
would be instrumental in promoting her reputation, and for some it was
very much in their own interest to do so.

In Catherine's lifetime, the holders of the papal office were all French.
In 1309, Clement V had moved the papal court from Rome to Avignon,
a move which in practical terms was eminently reasonable. By the
fourteenth century, the (papal) court had become a place of judicial
business and, as Richard Southern argued, if anything this functioned
better and more economically away from Rome.[13] But for devout people
like Catherine, who were steeped in a sense of religious history, the see
of St Peter could only be in one place, and this lay behind her unstinting

---

[12]   *Life of Catherine of Siena*, p. 205.

[13]   R. W. Southern, *Western Society and the Church in the Middle Ages*
        (Harmondsworth: Penguin, 1970), p. 133.

attempts to bring the papacy back to Rome. This came about only when Gregory XI, who in 1370 was the last Frenchman to be elected pope, proved himself to hold a similarly deep-seated belief that the pope's rightful place was in Rome.

Gregory's spiritual conviction was reinforced by a practical consideration. During the years of the Avignon papacy, the Papal States in Italy were in increasing turmoil and often in conflict with other states. Things came to a head in 1375, when papal officials refused to export grain to help relieve a famine in Florence. The city's authorities used this as a pretext to unite with neighbouring powers and to incite the towns of the Papal States to rebel. In May 1376, Pope Gregory sent Cardinal Robert of Geneva and a band of mercenaries to reconquer the Papal States in a war that became known as the War of the Eight Saints. This was the conflict in which Catherine tried unsuccessfully to engage William Flete (see below).

Catherine also managed to win Flete's support in advocating a new crusade, which she had allegedly prophesied would take place in her lifetime, an interpretation of prophecy which Raymond hotly disputed.[14] Raymond reports Catherine's visit to Avignon, and her conversation with Pope Gregory XI, when the pontiff told her: "The first thing we must do is to make peace amongst Christians; only then can we organize the holy Crusade", to which Catherine replied, "You will find no better way, Holy Father, of making peace amongst Christians, than by first organizing the holy Crusade."[15] William later echoed the argument that a crusade would bring a new unity in the Church in his letter to "the Friars of the Province of England", whom he urged to pray for the true pope (Urban VI), and for the "enlightenment of schismatics", concluding: "Pray, all of you, that the crusade may come about soon, and that we may all die there together for Christ."[16]

A few months later, the pope sailed for Italy. He arrived in January 1377 after a long and perilous journey, only to find his cardinals begging him to

---

[14]   *Life of Catherine of Siena*, pp. 266–72.

[15]   Ibid., p. 268.

[16]   Benedict Hackett, *William Flete, O.S.A. and Catherine of Siena* (Villanova, PA: Augustinian Press, 1992), p. 145.

return whence he came, because of the dangerous situation brought about by atrocities committed by Robert of Geneva's mercenaries. Gregory did not resist their request for long. But before he could leave Italy he died, in March 1378, a sign, some said, of God's displeasure at his weak will.

After Gregory's death, the cardinals came under pressure from the people to elect an Italian, who, it was thought, would not be tempted to move back to France. In the first conclave to be held in Rome for more than seventy-five years, they elected the Archbishop of Bari, a native of Naples who had nonetheless spent many years in Avignon.

The new pope, Urban VI, turned out to be violent and overbearing to a degree bordering on insanity.[17] Arguing that the threat of popular violence was tantamount to an election carried out under duress, the French cardinals declared Urban's election invalid and appointed Robert of Geneva in his place. Taking the name of Clement VII, the new pope— or, more correctly, anti-pope—promptly returned to Avignon. This marked the beginning of the thirty-nine-year Great Western Schism, an impossible situation which caused Catherine great anguish and which, of course, she would not live to see resolved. No one was spared in the division of Western Christendom that ensued. Catherine was unstinting in her support for Urban, the rightful pope, despite his evident failings. But other holy men and women were equally fervent in their support of Clement.

Behind the bare historical facts of the latter years of the Avignon papacy, Catherine's role in encouraging the pope's return to Rome should not be underestimated. Her persuasion on a spiritual level, perhaps even more than the increasing urgency of the political situation, had finally persuaded the deeply pious Gregory XI to make a move. With an extraordinary forthrightness, born of her conviction of her divine calling, she did not hold back. One of her letters in 1376, the year of the Florentine rebellion, begins after scant greeting:

---

[17] Eamon Duffy, *Saints and Sinners: A History of the Popes* (New Haven: Yale University Press, 1997), pp. 126ff.

> I long to see you a courageous man, free from any cowardice or
> selfish sensual love in regard to yourself or any of your relatives.[18]

She calls forcefully for Gregory to act decisively: "Up then, Father; don't
sit still any longer",[19] and her hints at his weakness are unmistakable.
"Regarding yourself", she writes, "try to go confidently."[20]

In spite of this, Catherine remains conscious that she is under papal
authority, and she often softens her remarks with protestations of her own
humility and unworthiness. Not so when she writes to secular leaders,
whom she was distressed to see turning against each other. To Charles V
of France, referring to his conflict with Louis, Duke of Anjou, she says:

> What an abomination before God that you should be making war
> against your brother and leaving your enemy alone . . . Enough
> of this stupid blindness![21]

while in a letter to Louis she is critical of his luxurious lifestyle and urges
him to "make . . . an effort to amend your life".[22]

However harsh her words may be, Catherine never loses sight of her
conviction that they are from God. Her letters to Pope Gregory are full of
biblical imagery and at times read more like sermons. She is particularly
fond of the image of sheep and the shepherd (good or bad) and appeals
to the pope to follow the example of Christ and the apostles. Even so, a
hint of reproach remains:

> I long to see you a good shepherd . . . for I see the infernal wolf
> carrying off your little sheep and there is no one to rescue them.
> So I am turning to you, our father and shepherd, begging you in
> the name of Christ crucified to learn from him who with such

---

[18]   Suzanne Noffke, O.P. (ed. and tr.), *Letters of St Catherine of Siena* (New York:
       Paulist Press, 1988), p. 222.

[19]   Ibid., p. 217.

[20]   Ibid., p. 267.

[21]   Ibid., p. 239.

[22]   Ibid., p. 241.

blazing love gave himself up to the shameful death of the most holy cross to save this little lost sheep, the human race, from the devil's hands.[23]

But her full wrath is reserved for the pope's rivals back in Italy, the "bad pastors and administrators", who she describes as "devils incarnate" and fearful like Pilate "who killed Christ so as not to lose his authority".[24]

Catherine also used her way with words to offer encouragement and to promise her prayers. In her final letter to Gregory before he arrived back in Rome, she wrote:

> Let your heart rejoice, for in the many contrary things that have happened or will yet happen the deeds of God are surely being done.[25]

and she concludes:

> Find encouragement and confidence in the true servants of God—I mean, in their prayers, for they are praying and interceding much for you. I humbly ask for your blessing, and so do your other children. Keep living in God's holy and tender love.[26]

Catherine's letters make it clear that she is fearless in speaking on her own authority. This is in marked contrast to, for example, Margaret of Cortona, who is cushioned from the wrath of those whom she rebukes because she is delivering words explicitly given to her by Christ. A lengthy tirade conveying divine displeasure begins like this:

> It was the fifth day of May that Christ said to Margaret after Communion: "My child, I command thee to send word to the

---

[23]   Ibid., pp. 200–1.

[24]   Ibid., p. 205.

[25]   Ibid., p. 266.

[26]   Ibid., p. 267.

> Bishop of Arezzo that he must give up all those revenues of the
> Church which belong to the poor, and that he must not league
> himself with the factions which divide the people of Tuscany
> . . ."[27]

Maybe conscious of the need for similar diplomacy, Raymond notes that Catherine dictated her *Book* (and maybe by implication, her letters) under the inspiration of the Holy Spirit: "This was the Lord's work, making clear to us that the volume was not composed by mere natural power, but by virtue of the Holy Spirit."[28]

Wider connections

Catherine's later appeal outside her own country has never been in doubt. Her spirituality would create a natural bond with other women and movements across the continent, and already in her lifetime she was attracting like-minded people from outside her homeland to join her in her endeavours.

An English connection: William of Flete

The Lincolnshire village of Fleet lies in the fenlands of South Holland, at the mercy of the winds that sweep in from the Wash. It is an ancient settlement, recorded in the 1086 Doomsday Book as Floet (meaning stream), and by the fourteenth century its name was appearing as Flete. Today Fleet would be indistinguishable from its neighbours, were it not for its distinctive church, one of a number in the fens whose architectural magnificence tends to catch the traveller by surprise. Dedicated to St Mary Magdalene, Fleet Parish Church is remarkable for its detached tower, which stands noticeably apart from the church itself, a feature not uncommon in marshland where the presence of a heavy tower attached to the main building might cause subsidence of the church itself.

---

[27]   Fr Cuthbert, *A Tuscan Penitent*, pp. 119–20.

[28]   *Life of Catherine of Siena*, p. 310.

At about the time the church was under construction, a young man left the village to study theology at the University of Cambridge, some fifty miles away. William was born around 1325, and when he was about fourteen, he entered the Augustinian Order.[29] He studied theology in his Order before being sent to university to read for an MA, although he never took his degree. In February 1352, he was licensed to the diocese of Ely. Then, in July 1359, William left England for Siena with two companions, resolved never to return to the country of his birth.

The reason for William's self-imposed exile seems to lie in a spiritual quest for isolation rather than in any desire for the good things of life that Tuscany had to offer. In that he was anticipating the actions of two other East Anglians: Mother Julian, who from around 1373 found isolation from the world by being shut away in a cell in Norwich; and Margery Kempe who, some forty years later, would abandon her husband to journey with strangers to the Holy Land. In seeking spiritual enrichment by cutting himself off from his homeland, William seems to have been following something of a trend among Friars of his time.[30]

William (or Brother William of Anglia, as he called himself) settled in Lecceto, nine kilometres west of Siena. Formerly a Benedictine foundation, and still today a place of pilgrimage, Lecceto had been Augustinian since 1244, when Pope Innocent IV granted the necessary dispensation from observance of the Rule of St Benedict. Legend has it that Augustine had visited Tuscan hermitages in Pisa and Lecceto around 387-88, presumably on his journey from Milan, where he had been Professor of Rhetoric, back to Africa, where he became Bishop of Hippo a few years later. So for William, Lecceto represented the home of the Augustinians outside North Africa, a place where the tradition of the Order's founder was uniquely preserved. This would have been important to him in view of the general decline of religious Orders in England and the relaxation of earlier standards of austerity. One aspect

---

29 Biographical details in B. Hackett, O.S.A., *William Flete, O.S.A., and Catherine of Siena* (Villanova, PA: Augustinian Press, 1992).

30 See A. Gwynn, S.J., *The English Austin Friars in the Time of Wyclif* (London: Oxford University Press, 1940), quoted by Hackett, n. 29 above, p. 23, n. 6.

of this was the Friars' gradual absorption into academic life which he had encountered at Cambridge.[31]

William did not meet Catherine until he had been in Lecceto some nine years, at the very earliest. By then he had built up a considerable reputation as a spiritual counsellor, with particular expertise in the problem of temptation. Before leaving home, he had written a short treatise on the subject, and this became a popular piece of spiritual writing in the late Middle Ages in England. "How strange and various are the ways in which the soul of one who fears God is harassed and battered", William had mused there,[32] and the appeal for Catherine of such a way of thinking is not hard to gauge.

Catherine paid her first visit to Lecceto in 1367, and thereafter, maybe for as long as six years, the English Augustinian Friar was an important influence on her theological thinking, until in 1374 William was replaced by Raymond of Capua as her confessor. Catherine and William had much in common, not least their shared conviction that the way to salvation lay in the contemplative life, which could be brought to perfection through works of charity. William has been credited with introducing Catherine to some distinctive Augustinian ideas which would emerge in her own writing, most notably her teaching on knowing oneself and God.[33]

William's influence in Siena extended beyond his role as a spiritual counsellor. Various letters to the city's governors show him to have been actively involved in local politics. (So much for seeking isolation.) Hackett even speculates that he may have been instrumental in enabling two of Catherine's brothers (who had supported the overthrown rulers known as The Twelve) to escape Siena unhindered after the 1368 revolution and to find safety in Florence a couple of years later.

William's association with Catherine did not end when Raymond of Capua was installed as her confessor. In January 1377, he wrote, at her dictation, her *Spiritual Document*, a short text in which Catherine,

---

[31]   See John R. H. Moorman, *A History of the Church in England* (London: Adam & Charles Black, 1953), pp. 144ff.

[32]   "On remedyes against temptation", 27, reproduced in *William Flete and Catherine of Siena*, pp. 127–38.

[33]   *William Flete and Catherine of Siena*, p. 87.

referring to herself in the third person, describes how she countered self-love with self-knowledge, which "resulted in such a hatred of herself that she sought nothing according to her own will, but only according to the will of God, which she knew was always for her good".[34] At the end of the document, William adds: "If this discourse were published and disseminated throughout the whole of our Order, I think that it would do a great good."

Another revealing document is an undated letter to Raymond from William, writing in his capacity of Catherine's confessor at the time.[35] It is a powerful eulogy. William writes about Catherine's gifts, which he considers to be underestimated, and compares her to Judith: "With the sword of her words she will cut off the head of Holofernes." It is not clear what provoked the letter. Perhaps William was formally handing over Catherine's spiritual care to his rival, or perhaps he was responding to criticism of her by Raymond or from some other source.

In 1379, there appears to have been some estrangement between William and Catherine. In that year, Pope Urban VI, who had been elected in 1378, included William's name in a list of eight leading religious figures whom he summoned to Rome to support him, a ploy which Hackett has little hesitation in attributing to Catherine. But William remained true to his calling as a Friar Hermit and refused to leave Lecceto. Catherine then wrote to him, urging him to accept this as God's will, and although William did at first agree to come, he eventually decided against it. In a letter to William's friend, Anthony of Nice, Catherine refers to his decision in scathing tones: "Obedience to God does not draw us away from this obedience (namely, the pope). Indeed when obedience to God is the more perfect, this obedience is the more perfect."[36]

However bitter the disagreement between the two may have been at the time, it did not sour their relationship for long. Before she died Catherine reaffirmed her confidence in her English friend, and in 1382, on the second anniversary of Catherine's death, William wrote a powerful "sermon" (see Chapter 10 below) in which he commended Catherine's

---

[34] Reproduced in ibid., pp. 181–4.

[35] Reproduced in ibid., pp. 167–75.

[36] Ibid., p. 95.

suffering on behalf of the Church, and referred, among other things, to her own extreme physical pain.

William outlived Catherine by some ten years. Hackett comments that he represents the only direct link between the fourteenth-century mystics of England and Italy. More significantly, though, his is the first testimony to the future patron saint of Europe that can genuinely be said to have a European origin.

It was, however, only a few decades later (*pace* Hackett), around 1420, that a Middle English translation of Catherine's *Dialogo* came into circulation. Based on a Latin translation by Cristofano di Gano Guidini, one of Catherine's scribes, this came to be known as the *Orchard of Syon*. Situated on the main road from London to Windsor, Syon Abbey was the pre-Reformation home of the newly arrived Bridgettine Order and achieved a certain notoriety when the bloated body of Henry VIII, en route to burial at Windsor, allegedly exploded there while its escorts were resting. As the English title suggests, Catherine's work is now presented as a more general model of female sanctity for the edification of English communities and laypeople. By contrast, when Raymond's *Life* appeared in English in the 1490s as the *Lyf of Katherine of Senis*, it was shortened and edited, possibly to better accommodate an English spirituality that tended to shun engagement with the affairs of the world.[37]

The French connection: Anthony of Nice

Anthony of Nice shares two notable dates with William of Flete. Like William, Anthony arrived at Lecceto in 1359, and he too died in 1390. A French Augustinian, he was a close friend of William's and a trusted associate of Catherine. And as mentioned above, it was to Anthony that Catherine addressed her letter of 1379 expressing her disappointment at William's failure to travel to Rome, knowing that the message would be passed on.

---

[37]   See further, Lisa Tagliaferri, *Lyrical Mysticism: The Writing and Reception of Catherine of Siena* (doctoral dissertation, City University of New York, 2017), available at <https://academicworks.cuny.edu/gc_etds/2154/>, accessed 25 September 2021.

Sadly, little is known about Anthony. The diocese of Nice includes him among a number of saints specially honoured in the diocese, listing him as "Blessed Antoine Gallus (1300-90), a native of Nice, one of St Catherine of Siena's confessors". Nonetheless, he is another European link in the chain of Catherine's relationships with spiritual leaders that stretches way beyond her native Siena.

Conclusion

Like Clare of Montefalco, Catherine's loyalty to the Church and the papacy was absolute. Yet the vastly different circumstances of the late fourteenth century meant that this loyalty took a rather different, and necessarily more public, form. Earlier mystics had been keen to promote their personal orthodoxy, and their biographers were key to this in recording the approval of local bishops and promoting their subjects' Christ-like activities. For Catherine and her followers, however, loyalty to the papacy was far from being a question of a little local difficulty. Loyalty meant intervening in a situation of national and international significance and struggling against all the odds to maintain an ideal of Christian peace and unity.

Catherine's reputation as a saint, established from a young age, enabled her to venture onto this international stage, confident that she was fulfilling a holy vocation. Yet it caused problems for her biographer, as the question of preaching a new crusade amply demonstrates. By now the original crusading spirit was a thing of a glorified past, its memory tarnished by the Fourth Crusade (that had diverted from its original purpose to become an attack on the Byzantine Church in Constantinople) and by the Albigensian Crusade of 1309, which not only wiped out a Christian heresy in the south of France but which at a stroke destroyed the flourishing culture and language of the whole region. Raymond of Capua's discomfort at having to deal with Catherine's enthusiasm for a new crusade is evident and reveals something of the challenge in creating an iconic figure who will promote the reputation of the whole Dominican Order as well as his own. However, the challenge of the creation of an icon is one that Sienese art and some of the greatest Italian artists in the future will embrace with notable success.

CHAPTER 7

Painting a picture: Conceptualization in art

As already suggested with reference to previous holy women, it is the choices made by artists that significantly determine how a saint will be perceived for years and centuries to come. These choices may be simple and obvious: for example, always portraying Catherine in a Dominican habit, which enables swift identification of her and her context, or showing her in the company of saints and martyrs as a sign of her own holiness. Or they may be more subtle: for instance, portraying her receiving the stigmata in a pose which is already reminiscent of St Francis and elevating her experience accordingly.

The subjects which the artist chooses are also important. If a saint is shown engaging in acts of charity, that is how he or she will be remembered. If, however, their activities are harder to visualize, then the artist will highlight an event that allows room for creative imagination. This is the case with Catherine's vision of a mystical marriage, which receives only a brief mention in Raymond's *Life*, but readily lends itself to a varied interpretation, as well as echoing art that depicts Katherine of Alexandria's experience of the same phenomenon. In addition, as highlighted in Chapter 2, the flowering of Italian art, in particular Sienese painting, in the years following Catherine's death was surely a key factor in establishing and promoting a view of her as a woman of special holiness.

Portrayals of Catherine
Characteristically Catherine is represented wearing the black and white habit of the Dominicans. Typically, she holds a lily, usually slanted across

one shoulder like a soldier's rifle, and sometimes too she holds a book (typically red with a golden clasp). The earliest stylized portraits show her head tilted to one side, her eyes demurely downcast, her lips unsmiling. Yet there is a surprising amount of variation as artists adapt this model to their own purposes. The uncompromising Dominican black is frequently attenuated to shades of grey or even green; the white of the garment beneath often takes precedence, even to the extent that at times the black cloak is barely visible. Some artists give Catherine a white headdress, its generous folds very much in keeping with the evolving fifteenth-century style; sometimes she appears all in white. When the figure is shown in action or at prayer, the lily and book may be laid beside her.

The symbolism of the lily is threefold. Basically, it indicates purity, and representations of the Annunciation sometimes have a vase of lilies set between Mary and Gabriel. By extension the lily comes to symbolize devotion to the Virgin rather than, necessarily, female virginity. Filippino Lippi's painting of the Virgin and Child with SS Jerome and Dominic (c. 1485, now in the National Gallery in London) shows Dominic holding a lily in his left hand, sloping back over his left shoulder. In turn, the lily also indicates a follower of this saint, hence the pose common to both Catherine and Dominic in some late medieval and Renaissance art.

Simple figures of the saint, whether painted or sculpted, would have been created primarily for devotional purposes, a stimulus to reflect on Catherine's life as a model for young women to follow. Burke quotes a certain fifteenth-century Friar, Giovanni Domenica, urging girls to reflect on a number of female saints so that they might develop "a love of virginity, a desire for Christ, a hatred for sins, a contempt for vanities",[1] and no doubt there were many depictions of Catherine that fulfilled this purpose. Inevitably some also have a didactic function, conveying information about events in the saint's life, yet may do so in such a way as to suggest something more profound. So, for example, in St Catherine's chapel in the S. Domenico Basilica in Siena, frescoes by Bazzi (known as Il Sodoma, 1477-1549) either side of the altar depict Catherine receiving the stigmata and Catherine in ecstasy. In both, Catherine is attended by

---

[1]   Peter Burke, *The Italian Renaissance: Culture and Society in Italy (1420–1540)* (1972) (revised edition, Cambridge: Polity Press, 1987), p. 127.

two women, also wearing the Dominican habit, while the presence of an ornate column rising up behind them makes both frescoes reminiscent of conventional poses of women at the foot of the cross, thus providing a strong hint of Catherine's devotion to the person of Christ.

Religious instruction and edification, therefore, is far from being an artist's sole purpose. Through art the subject may be elevated to new heights. Sodoma's implied comparison between Catherine and her attendants, and Mary and her companions at the foot of the cross, is a fairly subtle way of achieving this. Other artists are more obvious in their intentions; a favourite device is to add Catherine to their scenes of the Holy Family or to other episodes in the life of the Virgin. Girolamo del Pacchia (1477-after 1533) in a circular work in the Pinoteca of Siena shows a Holy Family with Catherine peeping over Mary's left shoulder, her lily crushed against the Virgin's back, but ignored by the main subjects. In similar vein, Neroccio di Bartolemeo Landi (1447-1500) has a *Mother and Child with SS Catherine and Bernard*. Catherine again looks over the Virgin's left shoulder, her lily following the line of Mary's head and neck. Bernard stands behind Mary to her right, looking across at Catherine, but again both are ignored by the Holy Family themselves. Matteo di Giovanni (1430/33-95) has a similar grouping, but with St Sebastian and an angel instead of St Bernard. Here Catherine is looking down at the child who is only just in her line of vision, and her red book is also visible.

Larger gatherings of saints are common in nativity scenes, in representations of the Virgin enthroned and in pictures of the Virgin's own birth. Working soon after Catherine's death, Paolo di Giovanni Fei (active 1372–1410) painted a triptych of the *Birth of the Virgin with Saints*, which includes among many others an obscured figure of Katherine of Alexandria on the left-hand panel and Catherine of Siena, also obscured, on the right-hand one.

The mystical marriage of both these saints is, of course, a good opportunity for artists to portray them either with the adult Christ or with the Virgin and the infant Jesus. Francesco Vanni (1563–1610) in his *Mystical Marriage of St Catherine of Siena* (now in the Pitti Gallery) shows an adult Christ with a remarkably youthful Mary beside him Catherine is kneeling, and Mary holds Catherine's right arm to receive the ring. The stigmata are clearly visible on Catherine's hands and her lily lies on the ground. Dandini's *Mystical Marriage* (in Siena Cathedral) also shows an adult, risen, Christ with his mother as Catherine receives the ring, while other artists imagine Catherine receiving her ring from the infant Christ.

With Katherine of Alexandria

In a study of 600 painters working in Italy between 1420 and 1540, Peter Burke has found that, despite a geographical bias to Tuscany and northern Italy, representations of Katherine of Alexandria far outnumber those of Catherine of Siena, making her the most frequently portrayed female saint of the Renaissance. Burke suggests that the explanation for this is Katherine of Alexandria's patronage of young girls, commenting: "Her 'mystic marriage' to Christ made her an appropriate subject for paintings given as wedding presents."[2]

The popularity of Katherine of Alexandria offers artists a happy means of enhancing the reputation of their local saint. The earlier saint is, of course, readily recognizable by the wheel that is almost always shown with her.[3] She is typically young and beautiful and finely dressed, and in that regard is clearly different from Catherine of Siena, who at best appears gentle rather than pretty and always wearing a habit. But like the Tuscan saint, Katherine of Alexandria is also often seen holding a lily and sometimes a book, and the virginity and mystical marriage that were common to both would have been well known to Renaissance observers. So, by drawing attention to what the two saints have in common, artists create a close association between Catherine of Siena and her more famous namesake.

The association is complete in an altarpiece for the Charterhouse at Pavia in a chapel dedicated to both saints. Ambrogio Bergognone's *Virgin and Child with St Katherine of Alexandria and St Catherine of Siena* (c. 1490) (now in London's National Gallery) depicts the mystical marriage of both saints (see Chapter 1). To the left is Katherine of Alexandria, with flowing black hair, dressed in red and holding a martyr's palm, and

---

[2]   Ibid., p. 165.

[3]   This is generally quite stylized, although the early sixteenth-century fresco by Fra Bartolomeo, now in the San Marco Museum in Florence, shows the saint with a wheel made up of vicious blades.

the infant Christ is placing a ring on her finger. To the right, Catherine of Siena, in her Dominican habit and holding a lily, is waiting her turn. The child has a second ring in his left hand and the Virgin is already raising Catherine's right hand to receive it. The Tuscan saint, here with a particularly sweet face, is looking down to her right. The whole scene is viewed from below, and Katherine's wheel in the foreground rests at the foot of the Virgin's classically decorated throne, perhaps in acknowledgement of her greater sacrifice.

Stigmata

A polychrome wooden statue of Catherine by Neroccio di Bartolomeo de' Landi (1447–1500) destined for the Oratory of Saint Catherine in Fontebranda, on the site of the Benincasa family home, is remarkable in that it both recognizes the bitter dispute between Dominicans and Franciscans over Catherine's stigmatization and, unlike conventional images and as befits its setting, shows the saint as a young girl with a face that has at least a hint of beauty. Neroccio's Catherine holds a book but no lily.

Even so, this girl bears signs of stigmata but painted in the form of a multi-pointed star on her bare hands, and on the parts of her clothing that cover her heart and feet. With the stars resembling a painted tattoo, this is a gentle image which is very much in keeping with the saint's still child-like features and downcast eyes. It is also one which is almost guaranteed to appeal to the faithful, with its more naturalistic approach and the modification of images of stigmata which might otherwise instil fear rather than belief.

Raymond of Capua's account of the ecstatic vision during which Catherine receives the stigmata sets it in the church of S. Cristina in Pisa. Since Catherine describes Christ as leaning down from the cross, artists have shown this as a figure on a church crucifix, set at a slightly alarming angle, with red or golden rays emanating from the wounds directed onto Catherine's body.

A panel painted in oil by the Sienese artist Domenico Beccafumi (1486–1551), dating from around 1513–15, shows Catherine in ecstasy reaching out towards the tilted crucifix, while other Dominican women, seeing only the saint's reaction, look on bemused, one of them mimicking her hand gesture.[4] A third sits at a distance unmoved, lost in her own thoughts or asleep. An altarpiece of the Nativity in the chapel behind her has Joseph and Mary reaching out to the Christ child in a similar way, thereby creating a distinctive bond of holiness with Catherine.

Enhancing reputations: Catherine and the city

Siena's Palazzo Pubblico (town hall) is home to a spectacular collection of artworks, many of them with themes that are eminently well suited to a former seat of government. One of the most notable are frescoes by Lorenzetti entitled *Allegory of Good and Bad Government* painted between 1338 and 1340 which occupy three of the walls of the Room of the Nine, also known as the Room of Peace. Adjacent to this is the Map Room, the meeting place of the Council of the Republic, which is dominated by Simone Martini's *Maestà* (1315, restored 1321), a picture of the Virgin and Child which is remarkable for its warmth and humanity. This transition from the secular to the sacred is completed by three archways leading into the chapel. Each pillar supporting the arches is decorated with images of local saints and holy men, who were no doubt intended also to promote the image of Siena. On one of the two central pillars is Lorenzo Vecchietta's *Saint Catherine*.[5]

This is a remarkable work on two counts. First, it was painted in 1461 and may well be the first representation of Catherine after her canonization (on 28 June of that year). Second, the figure of the saint is painted so as to give the impression of a statue in an alcove. She appears mainly in white, with, on the back of her hands, red stigmata, spider-like in appearance, that echo the colour of her Bible. Apart from the work's crucial position in the home of the Sienese government of the day, the figure herself resembles a typical Sienese painted wooden statue. Thus the person of the saint cannot be prised away from her Sienese context, either

---

[4]   Currently in the J Paul Getty Museum, Los Angeles.

[5]   Lorenzo di Pietro (Il Vecchietta) died in 1480.

in art or in reality. Even as Siena honours her, so Catherine enhances the reputation of the city itself.

Enhancing reputations: Catherine and the popes

Catherine was canonized by Pius II, a Sienese pope, whose life is commemorated in a series of frescos by the Perugian artist Bernardino Pinturicchio (c. 1454–1513) and his pupils in the Piccolomini library in Siena Cathedral. Aeneas Silvius Piccolomini was a poet and politician who initially aligned himself with the cause of the Avignon pope before being ordained priest at the age of forty-one. Having transferred his allegiance to Pope Eugenius IV he was made a bishop within a month of his ordination and became pope himself thirteen years later. In 1459, he took up the cause which had been close to Catherine's heart by proclaiming a crusade, this time against the Ottoman Turks.

The ninth fresco in the Piccolomini library shows Pius II canonizing Catherine. The primary focus is on the pope himself, who sits on his throne with some seemingly uninterested cardinals in attendance, while the saint's body lies at the foot of the steps leading up to the throne. Another point of interest in this brightly coloured and far from static fresco is one of the figures among those milling around in the foreground, which is thought to be a portrait of the young Raphael. Vasari describes the scene in these terms: "Aeneas places in the catalogue of the saints (or canonizes, as is said) Catherine, the Sienese nun and holy woman of the order of Preaching Friars."[6]

The purpose of the frescoes, though, is above all to enhance and preserve the reputation of the pope from Siena, which they do magnificently. And acknowledging Catherine as a saint is seen as the culmination of the career of Pius II before the tenth and final scene that represents his own death.

So the artists both help to create the reputation of Catherine herself and in turn use her to affirm the status of both her city and the papacy.

---

[6]   *Lives of the Artists* (Penguin Classics), pp. 251–2.

PART IV

Creating an image and spreading the story

Introduction to Part IV

> Texts were not stable; their precise meaning varied according
> to the company they kept, they were supplemented by cults and
> calendars, and more than anything they belonged naturally to
> wider bodies of stories about saints.[1]

James Palmer's warning about the interpretation of the written lives of
early medieval saints applies equally to the work of artists, and to non-
hagiographical compositions, from medieval epic to modern fiction. And
it is not simply to do with the ever-changing context of writers and artists,
although that is a key part of it. Their purpose in creating their own works
is all-important: enhancing the importance of local areas (Siena is the
example *par excellence*) and their patrons, who are depicted alongside the
holy ones; promoting themselves or the traditions of which they are a
part (for example, raising the profile of Franciscan or Dominican saints);
or upholding the tradition of the Church (as did Clare of Montefalco in
challenging heresy).

This process is far from straightforward. For example, when a
Dominican biographer chooses to emphasize the Dominican credentials
of his subject, he is doing more than simply promoting the interests of
his Order. Consciously or unconsciously, he is bringing someone whose
spirituality and activities lie on the margins of established religious
practice into the mainstream.

Thanks to their origins in a very limited area and their emergence
in a relatively narrow time span, the stories of the Tuscan mystics could
be viewed collectively as a model for the conceptualization of holiness.
Importantly, though, this is a living model, as new characteristics come

---

[1] James T. Palmer, *Early Medieval Hagiography* (York: ARC Humanities Press,
2018), pp. 60–1.

to be incorporated into their individual lives and into the purposes of those who portray their lives. These saints owe their image, as we currently perceive it, both as individuals and as a collective whole, to changes in the external context of their storytellers (such as the growth of anti-clericalism or the emergence of feminism) and in their individual creative purposes.

So, with the passing of time, there may emerge a reconceptualization of the holy ones. The twentieth-century theological preoccupation with the humanity of Jesus Christ rather than his divinity is reflected in a popular desire to portray the historical saints as more "like us". Preachers and teachers focus on the human failings of the apostles, in an effort to reassure us that redemption is within reach of us all. The presentation of Margaret of Cortona as a second Magdalene, a sinful woman, thus tends to take precedence over everything else in her life story. Contemporary or near-contemporary writers invite us to explore our own longing for forgiveness through Margaret's story, resulting in the near-secularization of the saint. An obsession with "making relevant" leads too readily to a watering down, an excessive generalization of individual saintly life courses.

Writers, artists and the Church all have a role to play in establishing, repeating and modifying the reputations of the medieval Italian mystics. And their influence comes to bear both on individuals and on the wider group of holy women of which they are a part.

CHAPTER 8

Making use of scripture

> Margaret . . . was ever unwilling to manifest the hidden things
> revealed to her, unless forced to do so by a Divine command or
> persuaded by her confessor; or unless she was impelled to speak
> by fear of delusion, or because she thought that what she heard
> was not in accordance with the Holy Scripture . . . She would not
> presume to believe anything as true when it seemed to her to be
> in disaccord with the teaching of Holy Writ.[1]

Fra Giunta's insistence on Margaret of Cortona's attitude to scripture is not
only concerned with highlighting the orthodoxy of her beliefs and behaviour.
It is designed to place his subject firmly in the company of the saints of the
Gospels and thereby to reinforce arguments for her canonization.

Medieval writers were, of course, working in times when their
audiences were much more alert to biblical references than they are today.
Any comparison with scriptural figures and events, whether from the Old
or New Testaments, would have been full of meaning for people hearing
or reading the *vitae*, and they would have had little hesitation in drawing
mental parallels between, say, miracles associated with local holy women
and men and the miracles of Jesus. It therefore follows that biographers
are in a position to enhance the reputation of their subjects as much by
simple allusion as by lengthy comparisons.

In comparing Margaret the repentant sinner to Mary Magdalene,
Fra Giunta is following a well-established and well-understood pattern
that both highlights her repentance and forgiveness and ensures her
rehabilitation. The story of Pelagia of Antioch (see box) is an early
example of desperate repentance.

---

[1] Fr Cuthbert, *A Tuscan Penitent*, p. 71.

The prostitute Pelagia

The stories of Syrian holy women are mainly focused on the key events of conversion, Christian testimony and martyrdom. The attention given to female sexuality and the violence suffered by these women at the hands of men (see Chapter 1) largely precludes explicit scriptural parallels. However, insofar as the theme of repentance is concerned, the figure of Mary Magdalene is unmistakably present. The account of the conversion of the prostitute Pelagia of Antioch in the late fourth century exemplifies this. Invoking the encounters with Jesus of various women in the Gospels, beginning with the Samaritan woman (John 4), Pelagia appeals to Bishop Nonnos for an audience with him, which is duly granted, with the proviso that seven other bishops should be present (we have already learned that Nonnos is more than a little taken with Pelagia's beauty). The story continues:

> As [Pelagia] drew near [to the bishops], she prostrated herself before them all together and ended by throwing herself down on the ground, clasping the feet of the holy Nonnos in a state of great emotion. She started to weep and groan, and the holy man's feet got soaked with the prostitute's tears. Without noticing what was happening, she wiped onto herself the dirt from his feet.[2]

Without explicitly mentioning the unnamed woman of the Gospels (Luke 7:38), the allusion to Jesus' feet being wiped by a woman's hair is unmistakable. Brock and Harvey comment that this text, written by Bishop Nonnos' chaplain, "deacon Jacob", became especially popular in the West during the Middle Ages,[3] in which case the writer's appeal to scripture, and also his shameless promotion of both his bishop and himself, are important pointers to the narrative preoccupations of later hagiographers.

---

[2]   Sebastian Brock and Susan Ashbrook Harvey, *Holy Women of the Syrian Orient* (Berkeley: University of California Press, 1998), p. 49.

[3]   Ibid., p. 41.

However, Margaret's story does not end there, as she goes on to experience other encounters with Jesus that are linked to Mary Magdalene. In one of her ecstatic visions, she is allowed to follow Christ along all the stages of his Passion, so that in the eyes of the citizens of Cortona she is living out a scene of terrible suffering. When that was past, she became "like another Magdalene drunk with sorrow"[4] and is so much in character that she demands of all the onlookers where Christ's body might be, and where he might be "hidden away". And while Margaret is not shown as a witness to Christ's resurrection, she is reminded by him that this was granted to her namesake:

> Behold Magdalene: to her did I show Myself in the Garden after
> my Resurrection in such way as I was already in her soul. But
> now I have put thee in the world to be a ladder by which sinners
> shall mount to Me.[5]

As is also the case with other holy women, certain feast days of the Church are for Margaret the trigger for ecstasies and visions, in particular the eve of St Mary Magdalene. On one such occasion Margaret's vision includes the creation of a daring biblical parallel:

> She beheld Magdalene the Blessed, most faithful of Christ's
> apostles, clothed in a robe as it were of silver and crowned with
> a crown of precious gems and surrounded by the holy angels.
> And whilst she was in this ecstasy Christ spoke to Margaret
> saying, "My Eternal Father said of Me to the Baptist: 'This is My
> beloved Son'; so do I say to thee of Magdalene: 'This is My beloved
> daughter'".[6]

Taking God the Father's words to his Son and applying them to Mary Magdalene, who is the model for Margaret's own holiness, should surely help to cast Margaret in the mould of a very special saint. Yet it is the

---

4   Fr Cuthbert, *A Tuscan Penitent*, p. 79.

5   Ibid., p. 104.

6   Ibid., p. 93.

figure of the repentant sinner that will always be associated with her. And it has to be said that Fra Giunta's insistence on Margaret's obsession with her former sinfulness does not in the end do much to challenge that.

Miraculous feeding

The Gospel accounts of Jesus' miracles are, of course, presented as much to reveal his divine nature as to illustrate his (healing) love for those around him. The same might be said of the miracles associated with holy women during their lifetime: on one level miracles of healing, in particular, are acts of love and compassion to people in need; and on another level they are indicators of the saintliness of the miracle-worker. If biographers tend to emphasize the latter, it is because of their interest in the future status of their would-be saint. It would therefore be wrong to assume that the preponderance of reputation-building miracles in the *Legenda* somehow implies any relative indifference to individual suffering.

In seeking to establish parallels between Christ and these human lives, the biographers tend to favour the most spectacular of miracles: feeding a significant number of people with next to nothing, or, to a much lesser extent, restoring an apparently dead individual to life. In both cases, the biblical events of Jesus feeding the 5,000 and raising Lazarus from the dead might seem too familiar to need any explicit endorsement from scripture.

Nonetheless, Ardenti feels it necessary to include a direct reference to the feeding of the 5,000 in his account of a feeding miracle by Umiltà da Faenza. Having "raised her eyes to heaven" (a favourite expression of Ardenti, which itself has biblical overtones) Umiltà prays that Christ, who fed 5,000 people with five barley loaves and two small fishes, might similarly multiply the small mouthfuls of bread that the sisters have. With this prayer answered, he notes that more pieces of bread were left over than were originally present.[7] On a previous occasion, Umiltà has already enabled a small piece of fish, enough for just two people, to be distributed to the whole community, although this miracle is presented as a reproach to the *celleraia*, who had deemed it impossible to share.[8]

---

[7]   Ardenti, *Life,* p. 35.

[8]   Ibid., pp. 29–30.

As already noted (see Chapter 4 above), Umiltà's feeding miracles mostly benefit only her own community, which is unsurprising given her cloistered existence. Her healing miracles as listed by Ardenti both before and after her death certainly work for the good of some individuals both within and outside her own setting. Yet the writer's matter-of-fact descriptions allow no room for scriptural allusions, and he has seemingly little interest in creating further parallels to enhance his subject's claim to holiness.

Multiplication of bread was, asserts Raymond of Capua, a fairly frequent occurrence in the life of Agnes of Montepulciano. On one occasion when the sisters had no bread at all, they found that someone had left four small loaves on their doorstep, enough for two of them to eat. At supper, Agnes initiates a rite of consecration: "taking the little loaves of bread into her sacred hands and giving thanks, she blessed and broke them and distributed them freely to those seated at table",[9] an action which results in the loaves increasing to such an extent that there was enough for the whole community with plenty left over. This action directly mirrors that of Christ in feeding the 5,000 (Luke 9:16–17), which allows the author to dare to attribute to Agnes the words and gestures of a priest at Mass.

An early version of this miracle happened when Agnes was still only a child. Wanting to feed the hungry children outside the monastery, Agnes demanded that one of the sisters should recheck the empty box where bread was normally kept. This she did and found it completely full, enough not only for the hungry children but for the needs of the sisters as well—a story of miraculous provision, if not yet one of miraculous transformation.

Not content with an implied reference to a miracle of Jesus, Raymond goes on to invite his readers to reflect on an Old Testament source, the multiplication of oil by both Elisha (2 Kings 4:2–7) and Elijah (1 Kings 17:12–16), and also an angel's gift of bread to Elijah (1 Kings 19:5–8). Raymond comments: "I leave these applications to you because the similarity of the deeds causes clarity" and concludes: "the Lord Jesus

---

[9]   Raymond of Capua, *Life of St Agnes of Montepulciano*, p. 40.

has made his spouse like himself in the oft-repeated miracle of bread."[10] From this it follows that a life lived in imitation of Christ is more than one that is characterized by self-denial, charitable works and so on. The life of a saint is also marked by divine intervention: the saint is allowed to perform miracles that reflect God's favour and the gift of a share in divine authority.

This is echoed in a later episode where Agnes changes water into wine. Like the wedding in Cana, this is not a case of desperate need: rather, that wine was lacking for a meal, and no one could find anywhere nearby to buy some. Again, like the marriage feast at Cana, the new wine is distinctive, being of a different colour and having an "incredible and unusual taste". Unlike the biblical precedent, however, the diners are moved to "praise the power of the Creator and the sanctity of Agnes". Raymond concludes: "Thus the virgin Agnes was commended by all for having imitated the first miracle of the Saviour and for being his true disciple."[11]

There are many examples of similar miracles in the life of Catherine of Siena, and Raymond devotes a whole chapter of his work to "The miracles which the Lord worked through her on things inanimate" (Part 2, Chapter XI). There are, however, cases of miracles with a difference: where transformation takes place without Catherine being physically present.[12] In one instance, a miracle has healing as a consequence. This is when Catherine's "prolonged ecstasy" results in her suffering a series of fainting fits. In seeking a cure for her, Raymond himself calls for a special kind of wine, *vernaccia*, said to have healing properties, but a neighbour has only an empty cask, until, that is, the cask is opened and found to be miraculously full. Presumably the wine provided the cure, but at a cost of great distress to Catherine herself, when she hears people describe her as "one who drinks no wine herself, but can by a miracle fill with wine an empty cask". She turns to prayer and the result is a second miracle that cancels out the first. The wine in the cask, which had not been reduced

---

[10]　Ibid., p. 43.

[11]　Ibid., pp. 75–6.

[12]　There is a precedent for this in several healing miracles of Jesus, but Raymond makes no reference to them.

despite numerous citizens drinking from it, suddenly became thick and undrinkable. Result: disappointed citizens but a jubilant Catherine, because "her Spouse had rescued her from public praise".[13]

Raymond also recounts a feeding miracle that happened after Catherine's death in Rome, when Catherine's head was received back in Siena. Following Divine Office, it transpired that there was not enough bread to feed all the Friars and visitors who dined together afterwards. The visitors were served first, leaving only a little bread in the pantry for the Friars, until "through the merits of Catherine the bread was multiplied by divine providence, both on the tables and in the pantry, with enough to spare". After the meal Raymond makes a speech, telling the guests:

> She [Catherine] would not consent, at her own celebration, to leave us short of a miracle of the kind which was a favourite one with her while she was still alive. During her lifetime while she was still among us, she worked this kind of miracle repeatedly; and now she has worked it once again to show that she is with us still and is pleased with our homage. Let us give thanks to God and to Catherine.

Following this somewhat unnerving experience of the saint being present at her own wake, Raymond is led to reflect that Dominic had also provided bread miraculously in his lifetime. And he concludes, " . . . so Catherine, as being his daughter in a special sense, showed her perfect resemblance to her Father by imitating him in all her works",[14] which is an interesting way of elevating both Catherine and the founder of their Order as holy people to be imitated, thanks to their Christ-like miracles.

Manna from heaven

In the Old Testament, manna is a gift from God to his people in their wilderness years. In Exodus 16, manna has a dual purpose: it is food for the people but at the same time it is a test of their faith, as they are commanded not to try to store it overnight. It is described as "a fine flaky

---

[13] *Life of St Catherine of Siena*, p. 285.

[14] Ibid., p. 283.

substance, as fine as frost on the ground" (Exodus 16:14), and it is this that informs Raymond's description of the manna that frequently descended on Agnes. This manna, however, is not a source of nourishment. Rather, it is a sign of God's favour, a sign that her prayers are pleasing to him. And unlike the biblical manna, it is sweet smelling, and its flakes, which are described as being like snow, all bear the sign of a cross. On the day when Agnes takes the veil the whole church is filled with it, again a sign of God's favour.[15]

When Catherine of Siena visits Agnes' body, she too receives the gift of manna, which rains down on them both. It is a miracle that Raymond is quick to interpret and to claim authority for:

> Agnes, knowing that Catherine was to be her own companion afterwards in heaven, began to make her her companion, and to honour her, whilst she was still on earth, sharing with her what had been a characteristic sign of her own sanctity. It was a significant token: to all who had eyes to see, that the manna by the whiteness and by the minute sign of its grains, signified purity and humility, two virtues which shone out in a special way in the lives of these two virgins. This indeed I am myself in a better position to attest than anyone else, for I am the one who have written as best I could the *Lives* of both these virgins, a privilege granted me not for any merits of my own, but only by the sheer mercy of my Saviour.[16]

The manna that features in these *Lives* is a far cry from that described in Exodus. It is not a source of food, nor does it turn mouldy overnight. Indeed, people are able to gather it up and display it as proof of a miracle. There is no test of faith involved; instead it is a concrete indication of holiness and Raymond does not hesitate to use it as such and to associate himself closely with it.

---

[15] *Life of St Agnes of Montepulciano*, pp. 21–3.

[16] *Life of St Catherine of Siena*, p. 303.

Christ-like healing

Jesus tells the disciples of John the Baptist: "Go and tell John what you hear and see: the blind receive their sight, the lame walk, the lepers are cleansed, the deaf hear, the dead are raised, and the poor have good news brought to them" (Matthew 11:4–5).

Exercising unusual subtlety, insofar as he refrains from creating an explicit parallel, Raymond of Capua draws together various healing episodes to form a Christ-like image for Agnes of Montepulciano. In the final section of his *Legenda*, which argues the case for canonization, Raymond recounts a string of miracles that are associated with Agnes after her death: a couple of blind women regaining their sight (Chapter 7), lame people walking (Chapter 8), people unable to speak having their speech restored (Chapter 9), demons being cast out (Chapter 10) and prisoners set free. While there are examples of other forms of healing, including several resurrection miracles, described elsewhere in the book, this accumulation of miracles creates an unmistakable Christ-like image.

Raymond's description of Catherine's miracles after her death is rather different, although the message of holiness that he conveys is similar. Being close to the events himself, Raymond is able to include details about the recipients of the miracles and of their conditions, thus creating little stories within his main narrative and avoiding the more formulaic style of Agnes' biography. The miracles include the healing of a woman's paralysed and wasted arm, the face of a young girl being cured of leprosy and a woman who was blind in one eye recovering her sight after Catherine had appeared to her maidservant with an instruction that her mistress should attend church. In this last instance, Raymond cannot resist drawing his readers' attention to the example of Christ:

> Take note here, Reader, how Catherine acted. In what she did here she imitated her divine Bridegroom . . . This time she was not satisfied with curing merely the body of the one who invoked her aid, but desired to remedy the condition of her soul as well.[17]

---

[17] *Life of St Catherine of Siena*, pp. 354–5.

This, Raymond notes, was "our Saviour's way too . . . To those who came to him for bodily cures he first forgave their sins. 'Be of good heart, son', he would say, 'your sins are forgiven you.'"[18]

Raymond's accounts of the miracles performed by both Agnes and Catherine are markedly different from Lombardelli's *Lives*. Typically, Lombardelli devotes a chapter to miracles towards the end of each *vita* but with little detail and no scriptural references. In the case of Aldobrandesca, the relevant chapter is sandwiched between one where Alda predicts her death and her death itself. There is then a list of some sixteen healings, all brought about almost instantly by Alda making the sign of the cross over the sufferer. Apart from one instance of a blind woman regaining her sight and another woman being cured of evil spirits, the sufferers have fevers or unspecified pain.

It is worth emphasizing how Raymond's portrayal of the two Tuscan saints sets them apart from other holy women whose activities are treated so routinely. While Raymond is interested in, and has access to, the personal details of the people involved, which adds to the attraction of his stories, it is above all his use of scripture that separates his women from the rest, to be numbered with the saints.

The biographer and biblical writers

For the most part, biographers use scripture in this way in order to convey something of the holiness of their subjects and, if it is felt necessary, to confirm their orthodoxy in the eyes of the Church. As already shown, they may draw a direct parallel with a biblical figure or, most commonly, describe miracles and spiritual observances of the holy person that reflect the actions of Christ himself. With Raymond of Capua, however, and particularly his work on Catherine of Siena, comes a much broader appeal to scripture. He is not content to let readers draw their own conclusions from the events that he uses biblical parallels to present. He also draws on scripture to offer his own comments on Agnes and Catherine and to interpret their teaching. And most startlingly, at least by comparison with

---

[18]   Ibid., p. 355.

previous writers, Raymond sees the work of biblical writers reflected in his own approach to writing, which has the effect of elevating himself as well as his subject to a higher level.

The Second Prologue to Catherine's *Life* reads like a brief survey of Old Testament figures who referred to the action of writing. There is, from the Psalms, "Let this be recorded for a generation to come" (Psalm 102:18) and the cry of Job: "O that my words were written down! O that they were inscribed in a book" (Job 19:23), quotations that Raymond uses to justify his own activity:

> Reading these words of Scripture we must surely conclude that
> things which redound to the glory and praise of the name of God,
> and to the advantage of the whole human race, should be known
> and recorded not just within the narrow limits of their own time
> and place, but written down and spread broadcast to every future
> generation as well as their own.[19]

Moses, Samuel, Ezra and "other prophets" are all cited as having written inspired books, as, finally, are the Evangelists, "who were found worthy not only of preaching the Gospel, but of writing it down as well".[20] This is the tradition into which Raymond immediately places himself, in order to "record for all generations . . . the works which have been wrought by the Lord of power and glory".[21]

The Gospel of John provides Raymond with the opportunity both to strengthen his claim to veracity and to justify his apology for any omissions. Following Catherine's miraculous healing of a young man at Pisa, Raymond comments: "I was myself one of the witnesses in this case, so I can say with Saint John: 'He that saw it has given testimony, and his testimony is true'" (cf. John 21:24).[22] Later he calls on the Carthusian Prior of Milan to bear witness to the events at Catherine's death: "I can say, like John the Evangelist", he claims, "'He [the prior] is the one who

---

[19] Ibid., p. 19.

[20] Ibid.

[21] Ibid., p. 20.

[22] Ibid., p. 243.

knows that I am telling the truth.'"[23] Like the Evangelist, who concluded "there are also many other things that Jesus did; if every one of them were written down, I suppose that the world itself could not contain the books that would be written" (John 21:25), Raymond also comments, at the end of Part II, "There are many other wonders, too, which God worked by occasion of this spouse of his . . . which are not written in this book."[24]

It is, however, at the end of his *Life of Saint Agnes of Montepulciano* that Raymond's self-consciousness as a writer comes most clearly to the fore, when he dedicates his work to "the most high and incomprehensible Scribe [who] has written us all, O dearly beloved reader, in the book of life, by which and from which the knowledge in all books is derived".[25]

Offering interpretation: Creating etymology

An obvious device of artists in the late Middle Ages and beyond is to place local saints in the company of the great ones, who may be apostles or teachers or the Holy Family themselves. It is, however, also open to writers to establish their subject's holiness by association with those whose sanctity is beyond doubt. As already discussed, scriptural references play an important part in this, as do shared names—Katherine of Alexandria and Catherine of Siena, Margaret of Antioch and Margaret of Cortona, Agnes of Montepulciano and St Agnes of Rome. But a further device exploited by Raymond of Capua is the use of his own brand of etymology as a means of explanation and comment.

Raymond's *Life* of Agnes of Montepulciano opens with a reference to Jesus, the Lamb, who "chose spouses for himself from all eternity, unstained ewe-lambs".[26] This leads him to comment that in Agnes "we see a likeness to the Lamb; not only from virtuous works . . . but even from the very sound of her name, Agnes, we discern this likeness manifestly".[27]

---

[23]   Ibid., p. 318.

[24]   Ibid., p. 304.

[25]   *Life of St Agnes of Montepulciano*, p. 139.

[26]   Ibid., p. 3.

[27]   Ibid.

He goes on to explain that Agnes is derived from "Agnus", the Lamb, and "in everything, except for one vowel" the two names agree. So he deduces that Agnes must be a "ewe-lamb" (Agna), the spouse of the Lamb:

> For since names are imposed on things according to their properties, it would seem agreeable to the Lamb and appropriate to his spouse, united to him through the perfection of charity, to be called by a name united to his name. In this way, the sign is in accord with the thing signified.[28]

Although more recent linguistics would contest this view of semantics, there can be no doubt that Raymond was using language to establish from the outset a very special position for his subject. To cast doubts on her holiness would surely be tantamount to blasphemy.

Etymologically speaking, Catherine's name presents more of a challenge, but Raymond is up to the task. His First Prologue opens with a quotation from Revelation 20: "I saw an angel coming down from heaven, holding in his hand the key to the bottomless pit and a great chain" (Revelation 20:1). He goes on to suggest that the pronunciation of *Catharina* (sic) "when slurred" becomes *catena* (Latin "chain"), and claims that "it is the mysterious realities signified, and not the mere names of them, that basically correspond to one another".[29] This is followed by a convoluted and linguistically untenable argument that since the Greek *katha*, reflected in the first part of Catherine's name, means universal, and since "uni-versity" also includes the idea of "di-versity", this again indicates a chain, which is "a unity made up of diverse things". All this is designed to argue that a chain is formed by "inter-connected virtues" that are all contained in the name of Catherine:

> This need not surprise us, because our *Catharina* was one in whose heart were gathered together both the universal collectivity of all the virtues, which the Lord had granted her,

---

[28] Ibid., p. 4.

[29] *Life of St Catherine of Siena*, p. 9.

and the universal collectivity of all the faithful of the Church, which she loved so intensely.[30]

So Raymond, with his own version of nominative determinism, is able not only to state from the outset that Catherine was, like Agnes, special, because of another contrived association with scripture, but he also uses that to indicate the particular direction in which her sanctity will take her, namely to uphold the holiness of the Universal Church as well.

Furthermore, Raymond adds into this his own role as a writer, claiming that the passage from Revelation 20 "chimes in with this purpose of mine . . . giving it my own construction . . . and I cry out, to my own generation and to future generations too".[31]

William of Flete, who might already have been familiar with Raymond's argument, uses the same supposed derivation of Catherine's name but associates it with different biblical teaching:

> A chain consists of many links, and this servant of Christ is truly a chain of virtues. She possesses to an unbelievable degree the virtue of love of God and neighbour, and therefore hers are also all the other virtues; for the virtues are all interconnected, and in *love of God and neighbour consists all the law and the prophets* (Mt 22:40). Paul says that *love is patient, kind*, and so forth (1 Cor. 13:4). Likewise, Catherine is most kind and most patient in her sufferings.[32]

However, William has an alternative (and equally untenable) derivation to offer as well: "This name is formed from two words, *cata*, which means 'all', and *ruina*, which means 'ruin' or 'falling down'." This he considers particularly apposite because Catherine "throws herself down and prostrates herself on the ground for sinners", particularly in imploring

---

30   Ibid., p. 10.

31   Ibid., pp. 4–5.

32   William of Flete, Letter to Raymond of Capua, in Benedict Hackett, O.S.A., *William Flete, O.S.A., and Catherine of Siena* (Villanova, PA: Augustinian Press, 1992), p. 169.

God to have mercy on the Church and the Holy Father.[33] This second interpretation fits well with William's own agenda, which is to promote Church reform and to argue for a new crusade. He reinforces his understanding of Catherine "falling down for all" with a host of references to the work of the Holy Spirit, drawing particularly on the Gospels and on Pauline theology, as well as the Old Testament and Apocrypha.

Raymond the scholar

Raymond of Capua does not confine himself to scripture in establishing the holiness of his subjects. He makes extensive use of other external references, including the Church Fathers and later Doctors of the Church, as well as the Old and New Testaments. In the case of Catherine's *Life*, he is particularly drawn to the Psalms and to the Pauline epistles, but he also uses these sources in the interests of argument, or simply as part of his narrative style. At times it seems as though he is more concerned with his own cleverness than with his subject.

In Raymond's hands, even an apparently straightforward description of a vision can be used to create new insights. So, for example, when in the story of Agnes an unnamed "poor woman" receives a vision of Jacob's ladder, with its ascending and descending angels (Genesis 28:12), this provides the answer to the prayer of an heiress, the woman's benefactor, who is looking to spend her fortune appropriately. When Agnes arrives to establish her monastery, the heiress understands that her money is to be given to this endeavour. On this somewhat slender basis, Raymond is able to offer his own interpretation of the dream, building on a wider understanding that saw in the ladder a foreshadowing of the work of the Virgin Mary, who, as Raymond put it, in "touching heaven with the highest humility, she made God descend to earth, so that men could ascend to heaven". He continues:

> This vision, as narrated, clearly signifies the virgin Agnes, touching heaven by the work of sanctity, and by her merits

---

[33] Ibid., p. 168.

> inclining God to compassion toward those who invoke him and
> by her prayers aiding them to ascend to heaven.[34]

Not content with drawing a comparison between Agnes and the Virgin via Old Testament exegesis, Raymond moves Agnes to a new place, setting her now in the much wider context of salvation history. However, he can only do that by downplaying the angelic vision itself. By the Middle Ages, awareness of angels and speculation as to their nature had moved far beyond the confines of scriptural references. Raymond would surely have been familiar with the many commentaries on *The Celestial Hierarchy*, the sixth-century work by Pseudo-Dionysius, that incorporated angelic activity into the realms of theology and spirituality. As Steven Chase has noted, the functions of angels "encompass every conceivable aspect and nuance of the relationship between God and humanity".[35] Experience of angels was not restricted to a specific class of Christian. But for Raymond to draw a parallel between his subject and the work of the Virgin (symbolized by the angels on their ladder), that was something else entirely.

While Raymond's biography of Agnes is largely devoted to establishing his subject's holiness, in the case of Catherine he is at pains also to emphasize her own claims to scholarship, and this he does by reference to scriptural writing. Early on, in a description of Catherine's letters, Raymond aligns Catherine with the great letter-writer, St Paul: "[W]ho can fail to admire and to be amazed at the sublimity of their style and the depth of their doctrine, so admirably adapted to the ministry of saving souls?" he asks. Despite Catherine's ignorance of "the language of learning", Raymond comments that her style is "rather that of a Paul than of a Catherine. It is such as one would look for from one of the Apostles themselves rather than from an unknown young woman."[36]

Then a lengthy account of Catherine's own insights into Jesus' suffering in Gethsemane, which Raymond insists he has not heard from any other

---

[34]   *Life of St Agnes of Montepulciano*, p. 63.

[35]   Steven Chase, *Angelic Spirituality: Medieval Perspectives on the Ways of Angels* (New York: Paulist Press, 2002), p. 15.

[36]   *Life of St Catherine of Siena*, p. 6.

writer or speaker, offers him opportunity to reflect on her "wisdom and grace". Catherine argues that the words "Father remove this cup from me" have a double meaning, referring either to shrinking from death (which is a consolation to "timid souls") or to a lifelong yearning for the salvation of humankind (an encouragement to "heroic souls" to become ever more self-sacrificing).[37] When Raymond points out that the usual scholarly interpretation is that Jesus in his humanity instinctively shrank from the approach of death, Catherine tactfully replies that different people find in scripture what applies to them, rather than be burdened with a single interpretation. He then describes Catherine's further interpretation of the words that he has found in the records of her confessor Tommaso. Here Catherine refers to the words that follow, "nevertheless, not my will but yours be done", which are added to avoid any implication that *all* souls would share in the salvation procured by Christ's Passion: Jesus' prayer comes with a condition. And Raymond agrees that this is a scholarly explanation of Hebrews 5:7: "he was heard because of his reverent submission."[38]

In illustrating Catherine's teaching, and her words "at once well-chosen and rich in meaning", Raymond suggests that he too is able to learn from her interpretation of scripture, which, it must be assumed, is praise indeed.

Conclusion

While holy women themselves might incorporate biblical quotations into their speaking and writing as a natural part of their spirituality, their biographers have a far more utilitarian approach to scripture: to create or enhance the reputation either of the saint or of themselves.

At the most basic level, Fra Giunta's assertion of Margaret of Cortona's reverence for scripture serves to confirm the Catholic orthodoxy of her beliefs and to justify arguments for her canonization. Similarly, comparing her to the biblical figure of St Mary Magdalene effectively transforms her

---

[37] Ibid., pp. 198–9.

[38] Ibid., p. 200.

reputation as a sinner into that of a notable penitent. Raymond of Capua is much more subtle. He does not need to state openly that the miracles of Agnes and Catherine mirrored those of Christ himself: his readers would have no hesitation in making that association for themselves. And in so doing they were consciously or sub-consciously understanding the saints to be imitating the actions of Christ and being themselves recipients of divine power. Equally, holy women who are described or pictured as suffering the torments of the Passion cannot fail to be seen as special imitators of Christ.

Raymond also has little hesitation in finding biblical parallels for his own actions and using them to benefit himself and his Order, most particularly in appropriating the sign-off to St John's Gospel, which enables him to reinforce his claim to the truth of his narrative. His use of very short quotations from scripture as part of his narrative style also illustrates his personal knowledge and learning, as do references to scholarly works. As Chapter 9 will demonstrate, this is one way in which the biographer becomes part of the story.

Once the reputations of the holy women have been established, and they become accepted by the Church they cherish, the Church too becomes part of their story. And, as Chapter 10 will argue, the Church will also at times use these saints for her own ends.

CHAPTER 9

Presence and intervention

An apologia for Catherine, a manifesto for the reform of the Dominican Order, and a defense of the Roman line of popes in the Great Western Schism.[1]

Bernard McGinn's description of Raymond of Capua's *Life of St Catherine of Siena* is a fair indication of the extent to which the genre of the *vita* readily evolved to incorporate the biographer's (or his community's) own interests. It had almost always been the case that biographers intruded on their subject's story in some way or another, in order to promote a particular view of themselves or their subjects, or both. Chapter 1 has already highlighted instances of this in the stories surrounding Syrian women in the fifth and sixth centuries, where some storytellers are the companions of a notable holy man whose qualities they are just as interested in promoting as those of the women themselves.

Raymond's life of Catherine, by virtue of its sheer length, represents the culmination of this trend. It will also be the case that in building his picture of a saint about whom there were already many popular anecdotes in circulation, Raymond is necessarily selective, to the extent of excluding stories that fail to suit his purpose.

---

[1]   Bernard McGinn, *The Varieties of Vernacular Mysticism 1350–1550* (New York: Crossroad Publishing Co., 2012), p. 199.

Promoting the Order

When the biography of a saint is written by a member of the same religious Order, the temptation to take the opportunity to use her to enhance the Order's own reputation appears irresistible. This in itself is sufficient to influence the choices made in the narrative in terms of what is included and what is omitted. In addition, however, the biographers are far from being dispassionate observers. Having a formal relationship with the saint, most commonly as a confessor, is a source of pride for them; and this in turn seems to give them licence to introduce their own comments on events and their own interpretations of the subject's experiences or teaching. And equally irresistible, it seems, to a male biographer is the opportunity to express his views not simply on a particular holy woman but on the nature of women in general.

It is worth noting, however, that reminding readers of a particular Order was a strategy that misfired in the case of Umiltà da Faenza. Umiltà's biographer Silvestro Ardenti, a Vallombrosan monk, informs his readers that the monastery founded by Umiltà and dedicated to S. Maria Novella followed the Benedictine rule and was a Vallombrosan congregation,[2] while one of the miracles at Umiltà's tomb cures a Vallombrosan monk of a painful arm.[3] But, as Simonetti notes, Umiltà's model of holiness was tied to a monastic tradition that was fast losing ground to the irresistible growth of mendicant Orders,[4] which may well explain the saint's later obscurity.

Franciscans

> These things she related to me, her confessor . . . But having spoken thus, she turned to me with great spiritual joy and asked: "Dost thou wish, father, to go home to the Friars with a glad heart?" And when I replied that it was so, she said: "Know then from Christ himself . . . that the Holy Ghost dwells more fully in

---

[2]   Ardenti, *Vita*, p. 26.

[3]   Ibid., p. 53.

[4]   A. Simonetti, *I sermoni di Umiltà da Faenza*, p. xxx.

the brethren of thy Order than in any other body of people under heaven: for such Christ revealed to me."[5]

Since it was the Franciscans who offered sanctuary to Margaret of Cortona and subsequently admitted her to their Order, it is unsurprising that Fra Giunta should devote significant attention to the Order in telling Margaret's story. If this is propaganda, it is certainly bold propaganda, since it is mostly spoken by the Lord himself. Thus the Franciscans are a crucial presence from the start: "Bear in mind, *poverella*, how the beginning of thy soul's recovery was in that filial reverence which I put into thy heart towards the Friars Minor, to whose care I committed thee",[6] says Jesus, who goes on to describe the Friars as "my Elect whom I love with intimate affection".[7] The elevation of the Franciscan Order culminates in a virtual hymn of praise to St Francis himself, which is initiated by the Lord telling Margaret she is "my little plant whom I have planted in the garden of the blessed Francis". The somewhat astonishing words used also contain an apparent rebuke to critics of Margaret's devotion to the founder of her Order, and are followed by Margaret receiving a vision of Francis among all the saints:

> The Lord said: "Much in truth did I love [Francis], and much was I loved by him, and I tell thee it is very sweet to Me when men love his Order, because of him whom I have loved in all sweetness. Wherefore be not concerned because thy companion rebuked thee for what thou didst say in an excess of admiration that thy father St Francis was as a new god: for in some ways I have made him like to Me. For even as I had twelve chosen apostles, so he had and still has many chosen ones."[8]

However, Fra Giunta does not wholly exclude criticism of his Order, which is conveyed through the Lord's demand that Margaret should act

---

[5]   Fr Cuthbert, *A Tuscan Penitent*, p. 76.

[6]   Ibid., p. 36.

[7]   Ibid., p. 45.

[8]   Ibid., p. 67. St Francis is also known as *il poverello.*

as his messenger: "When [the Friars] preach they are not to talk about the birds of the air or otherwise vainly, but let them preach the words of the Gospels and the Epistles." If this was a complaint commonly made against the Friars, it is promptly attenuated by an affirmation of their superiority: "Tell the Friars that I have given them larger nets and greater power in preaching the Gospel than I have given to other preachers."[9]

Dominicans

In the hands of Raymond of Capua, the holiness of his subjects—Agnes of Montepulciano and Catherine of Siena—builds up and enhances the reputation of their Order while at the same time their close association with St Dominic is a significant contributory factor to the perception of their own saintliness. This dual focus is best seen in his recounting of the visions in which both women were led to choose the Dominican Order over the Franciscans and Augustinians.

In Catherine's dream (see p. 34 above), St Dominic is the only figure who is named among the "Fathers and Founders of the various religious orders"[10] and there is no contest. Dominic addresses Catherine as "Dearest Daughter" and brings her "perfect consolation" at a time when her longing for the religious life was in conflict with her family's desire to marry her off. In the case of Agnes, though, it is more than a matter of spiritual comfort and reassurance: it is an assertion that the Dominican Order is to be preferred above the rest.

Agnes' vision is of three "large and beautiful ships", one each for Augustine, Dominic and Francis:

> Each of them wished to draw the holy virgin to his ship, and especially Blessed Francis, who alleged that the habit which she at that time wore agreed totally with the habit of his sisters. After a long argument, Dominic, the glorious athlete of God, said to his companions: "It will not be as you say, but she will stay in my ship, because thus has the almighty Lord arranged."[11]

---

[9] Ibid., p. 105.

[10] *Life of St Catherine of Siena*, p. 50.

[11] *Life of St Agnes of Montepulciano*, p. 56.

There is a practical purpose behind this apparently unseemly squabble, and the angel who interprets Agnes' dream for her spells it out. Agnes was called to leave Proceno and found a monastery in Montepulciano. The angel tells her:

> Because the Friars Preachers do not have a priory in those places, the Lord in his great mercy has disposed that you submit yourself and your community to their care, so that through you the Order may be built up, not only by the female sex but also by male servants of the Lord, these servants being multiplied.[12]

The clear difference between Raymond's life of Agnes and his work on Catherine is that Raymond had not known Agnes; as he frequently reminds the reader, he was dependent on other people for his information about her, attaching particular importance to eyewitnesses. In light of this, the Dominicans have a special role in verifying some of the stories that Raymond includes. This is most striking in the accounts of miracles associated with Agnes after her death, which without such endorsement might have been dismissed as hearsay. In one episode, the mother of a child who was seriously injured in falling out of a pear tree reports her son's miraculous healing to "a venerable and religious man, who was very well known, Fra Jacopo da Laterina of the Order of Preachers, who at that time filled the office of prior in Agnes' monastery".[13] Fra Jacopo not only heard the woman swear to the truth of her story, which followed a dream of Agnes that she had had, but wrote the events down and corroborated them with his own testimony.

There is a similar story when a prisoner from Perugia is miraculously freed from jail on the eve of his execution. He prays to the Virgin, who promises that he will be saved if he invokes Agnes, of whom he has never heard. Once free he makes his way to Agnes' monastery where "he even swore to the whole narrative by means of the Friars Preachers",[14] and offers all his possessions to the monastery.

---

[12]   Ibid., p. 57.

[13]   Ibid., p. 107.

[14]   Ibid., pp. 132–3.

By using Dominicans to confirm Agnes' holiness, Raymond is able both to consolidate his subject's reputation and remind his readers of the importance of his own Order. While they have little to do with the main events of the biography—Agnes as a child is once described as sleeping on the floor like her "father-to-be Dominic" and before death she consoles her followers as Dominic had done[15]—the Dominicans seem to be never far away, thanks not least to Raymond's frequent references to himself as the writer. This is established from the start, in the book's Prologue where he exclaims:

> . . . let all of Tuscany exalt because it has been decorated with such a noble treasure. Also let the happy Order of Preachers celebrate, under whose correction and rule, by divine revelation, this brilliant star placed herself, as will be disclosed below. Let the Chapter of virgins of the monastery miraculously founded by this virgin be glad above all . . . and since it is built on such a firm rock and with such a strong arm, let it be securely confident that it is, in fact, secure.[16]

The elevation of the Dominican Order reaches an extraordinary climax when Raymond recounts Catherine's vision of St Dominic in dazzling glory. God shows her Dominic alongside Christ, and tells her that he is "the Father of these two sons; of the One by natural generation; of the other, by loving and affectionate adoption".[17] Unsurprisingly Catherine is amazed to see Dominic raised to "such a lofty height" and God goes on to explain the parallels between these two sons, declaring that "my special gift to him and to his Friars is understanding of the words I have spoken, and the grace of never swerving from them".[18]

Raymond introduces this episode with a reference to his own call to the Dominican Order, claiming that if he omitted this vision he would "show myself ungrateful to that great Father of mine who himself, in a

---

[15] Ibid., pp. 20, 88.

[16] Ibid., pp. 4–5.

[17] *Life of St Catherine of Siena*, p. 195.

[18] Ibid., p. 196.

manner which, if I must tell the truth, was nothing less than miraculous, called my unworthy self to join his Order".[19] So by juxtaposing something of his life story and Catherine's vision, Raymond is able to remind the reader of his own reputation as well as embellish that of the saint.

The biographer in the story: As confessor

Where a biographer receives his subject's story by way of dictation, there is necessarily a certain relationship between them. And where he is also that subject's confessor or spiritual advisor, the relationship is a close one, to the extent that eyebrows were sometimes raised about their propriety. In all those circumstances, writers cannot resist giving themselves a part to play in the narrative. At times they appear as a moderating influence when the holy women become excessive in their penitential practices. They may be the recipients of a message from God, transmitted by the saint herself. And they may even be alongside the saint in her work outside the walls of the convent.

As already noted, the importance of confessors grew considerably with the move towards more frequent receiving of Holy Communion by the laity. Women mystics who were devoted to the Sacrament became equally wedded to the practice of confession that preceded it. Conversely, confession was for the Church a means of checking on the orthodoxy of those whose communities were often only tenuously linked to an established monastic Order. And both the confessor-biographer and the mystic had a vested interest in a close relationship, as a result of which their respective reputations might flourish.[20]

---

[19] Ibid., pp. 194–5.

[20] The fascinating issue of power relations between confessor and mystic is examined by Janette Dillon in "Holy women and their confessors or confessors and their holy women? Margery Kempe and the continental tradition", in R. Voaden (ed.), *Prophets Abroad: The Reception of Continental Holy Women in Late Medieval England* (Woodbridge: D. S. Brewer, 1996), pp. 115–40. Dillon concludes: "Together [the female visionary and male confessor] combined the validation of the church on earth with the authority of divine revelation" (p. 137).

A notable example of this closeness is Angela of Foligno's scribe, her confessor and cousin, Arnaldo. As already illustrated (Chapter 3 above) Arnaldo often seems more concerned to protect his own and his family's privacy than with promoting his relative's reputation, along with her often excessive ecstatic experiences. He is at times puzzled by what she dictates to him, at times humbled by it, but his intervention in his text amounts to little more than seeking clarification of what he hears.

Nonetheless, Arnaldo's participation in Angela's story has an unusual starting point. A year after Angela's pilgrimage to Assisi, it seems that Arnaldo began to question Angela more fully about what had actually happened there and started to write down her experiences in order to discuss them with his fellow Friars, work which eventually became Angela's *Memoriale*. And while there is no desire on Arnaldo's part to produce a piece of writing that might lead to canonization, he became intimately involved in its creation. As Lachance puts it, "The role Arnaldo played not only as the dedactor [= redactor?] of Angela's story but also as her spiritual director and as a catalyst for growth was inestimable."[21] As confused relative, questioner, confessor and encourager, Fra Arnaldo is intimately connected with Angela's spiritual development in a way that other biographers, including Raymond of Capua, will not be.

The more usual and complex relationship between confessor and mystic is well illustrated by that between Margaret of Cortona and her biographer, Fra Giunta, who plays an increasingly visible role in her spiritual development.

There is, for example, a curious episode, that Fra Giunta recounts at some length, in which he urges Margaret to challenge certain of her friends about some unspecified vices on their part which God has made known to Margaret. Referring to himself in the third person, Fra Giunta puts several arguments to Margaret, but to no avail. Eventually he makes her a strange and unethical proposition: Margaret should tell him what those vices were, so that when the people in question next came to confession, he could question them accordingly. This they do, and "when

---

[21] Paul Lachance, OFM, *The Mystical Journey of Angela of Foligno* (Toronto: Peregrina Publishing Co., 1990), p. 9.

these people came to confess to him the confessor questioned them, and found that what she told him was true".[22]

The confessor's importance is later underlined by the words of Christ himself. Despite Margaret's frequent privileged access to the Lord, she is not permitted to use him as a substitute confessor. Given Margaret's insecurity about the extent of forgiveness already accorded her (see Chapter 3), this would have been hard for her to hear. But as she begins to confess her faults, Christ interrupts her saying, "not to Me alone shalt thou confess thy faults, but to thy confessor also. I would have thee remember the lepers and how I sent them to the priests to be cleansed."[23]

While this episode greatly increases the importance of Fra Giunta the confessor, this is not to suggest that it is not authentic. Rather, his choice not only to include it but also to recount it at length might be indicative of a certain self-satisfaction at having a specific role that is shared with Christ himself. This three-way relationship is reflected in a direct message to Fra Giunta in respect of a live issue of the day: the spiritual state and physical appearance of people who receive Communion:

> Tell thy confessor that I command him never again to give the Communion of My Body to any person, whether religious or secular, unless she first cease to paint or adorn her face ... and unless he [sic] be disposed to obey My commandments and to do My Will. For the Communion of worldlings and their lives are an exceeding offence to Me ... And tell Fra Giunta to prepare himself diligently when he says Mass, and to take comfort in adversity by recalling to mind how I suffered; and let him have a diligent care to conquer himself.[24]

Margaret's confessor is also aligned with the saint, not this time in her relationship with God, but in her fight against the Devil. Fra Giunta notes

---

[22] Fr Cuthbert, *A Tuscan Penitent*, p. 60.

[23] Ibid., p. 108.

[24] Ibid., p. 102. The careful use of pronouns suggests a gender divide (see further below): while men fail in the significant elements of religion (obedience), women's failings are seen in terms of their cosmetics.

that the "enemy of souls" had turned him against Margaret "because, as it seemed to him, she was indiscreet in her austerities".[25] Here the role of the confessor as urging moderation is only briefly alluded to—the main context is the endeavours of Fra Giunta to make peace between the warring citizens of Cortona, the only time in the *Legenda* when he takes centre stage. And even here, he is subject to the Lord's rebuke for not having first reconciled the citizens of Cortona with one another before seeking peace with neighbouring cities. Is the confessor here setting the record straight? Or identifying himself more closely with Margaret, who will in due course be seen herself as protector of the city?

Margaret's biographer-confessor is not abashed to include his subject's prayers on his behalf. On one occasion she is rebuked by Christ for not praying for her confessor, "for thou art much beholden to him". Margaret replies:

> "Willingly, Lord, do I pray for him, for that I know well how greatly I am beholden to him, and the more especially do I commend him to Thee now since never did he speak to me of Thee as he spoke today". "He spoke well of Me", replied the Lord, "because I spoke through him". And Margaret: "Truly, Lord, did I know that Thou wert speaking through him, to my great joy."[26]

Following Michel Foucault, Phyllis Culham makes the point that in confession, power shifts from the speaker to the listener. In the case of mystics, however, the confessor's power is challenged when words fail to convey the experiences of the penitents, meaning that the truth is withheld from their confessors and power reverts to the speaker.[27] Similarly, the more usual model of the confessor praying for the penitent

---

25 Ibid., p. 114.

26 Ibid., p. 104.

27 Phyllis Culham, "Gender and negotiating discourse: mediated autobiography and female mystics of medieval Italy", in B. K. Gold, P. Allen Miller and C. Platter (eds), *Sex and Gender in Medieval and Renaissance Texts: The Latin Tradition* (New York: State University of New York Press, 1997), pp. 71–89, here at pp. 77–8.

is reversed, as the penitent is urged instead to pray for her confessor and, in this case, assure him of God's favour. So, in her *Dialogo*, Catherine of Siena prays for both her confessors, Raymond and Tommaso da Siena, whom she refers to as "guardians and masters of my wretched weakness" (*infirma*); but she is not simply asking for God's blessing on their calling. Rather, it is also a prayer for herself, that she might show them due respect and holy fear, an indication, perhaps, of an awareness of her own higher calling.[28]

Defending orthodoxy and promoting the papacy

In moulding holy women into an image acceptable to the Church, biographers must create some defence of their orthodoxy. While the most obvious way of achieving this is to place heavy emphasis on the association between mystics and monastic Orders, the biographer can also integrate the concern for orthodoxy into episodes in his subject's life.

Raymond of Capua, in his life of Agnes of Montepulciano, is not particularly subtle in this respect. At times his special pleading is all too obvious. When Agnes builds a church on a site of "public indecency by sinful women", she is careful to seek her bishop's permission for this and for establishing a monastery under Augustinian rule, because, says Raymond, she is someone who is "entirely Catholic".[29]

More interesting is Raymond's treatment of an incident that he claims to have found in a *legenda*, where visitors to Agnes' monastery witness a miraculous sign of Agnes' special merits. These unnamed men, of unspecified origin, are described as "men of great penitential austerity . . . praiseworthy reputation and high sanctity".[30] With the high integrity of these witnesses thus established, Raymond goes on to recount how, at the meal table, a lovely and sweet-smelling rose appears at Agnes' place,

---

[28] Quoted in *Le preghiere di Caterina da Siena*, ed. Angelo Belloni (Rome: Città Nuova, 2011), p. 114.

[29] *Life of St Agnes of Montepulciano*, p. 60. The care of the monastery, Raymond adds, would be committed to the Dominicans.

[30] Ibid., p. 48.

a sign of the beauty of her charity. Raymond couples this with a rather different episode where Agnes, by prayerful intercession, helps to save the soul of a one-time murderer from the flames of hell, both praying for him herself and urging him to make his confession, which he duly does.

By arranging his narrative in this way, Raymond is able to establish Agnes' credentials in the eyes of the Church in two ways: first, by the presence of impeccable witnesses to a miracle attesting to her holiness; and second, by demonstrating how "her merits and the power of sacramental confession" worked together. He goes on to tell the reader that "from all these things you may be able to understand plainly how this precious lamp illumined *the whole Church militant* because the divine light abundantly and copiously fostered and nourished in her the oil of compassion and piety, of which she was full".[31]

Once the doctrinal acceptance of a biographer's subject is in place, she may then be used in the interests of the Church and the pope, particularly when the latter is in a vulnerable position.

Towards the end of his life of Catherine, Raymond describes Catherine's dealings, or some of them, with Pope Urban VI.[32] While it may seem that Raymond is, as McGinn suggests (p. 175 above), promoting the papacy, in his portrayal of Catherine there is a certain degree of self-promotion going on as well. The pope had written to Raymond, knowing that he was Catherine's confessor, asking her to come to Rome. Catherine's response was that she has been accused of "gadding about", but that she would come to Rome if it is the pope's express wish—a reply that seems to put Raymond in the position of defending the saint's reputation. The pope duly issues an order for Catherine to come to Rome, where she is invited to address the cardinals with some words of encouragement in view of the developing schism in the Church. Raymond summarizes Catherine's speech and then quotes the pope's answer:

> Look, Brothers, and see how blameworthy we are before God for being frightened. This weak woman puts us all to shame. I call her a weak woman, not to make little of her; but I want to emphasize

---

[31] Ibid., p. 51 (emphasis added).

[32] *Life of St Catherine of Siena*, pp. 310–12.

that she *is* a woman, and belongs to what is by nature the weaker sex, and from that I want to draw a lesson for ourselves. By nature, it is she who should show fear, even in a situation where we would feel no danger. But, on the contrary, it is we who play the coward, while she stands undaunted, and by her rousing words imparts to us her own courageous spirit.[33]

It may be significant that the pope's words are reported directly whereas Catherine's are only alluded to indirectly, albeit in generous terms ("With an easy flow of language she put before them a courageous stand, pointing out how God's providence protects us always but especially at times when the Holy Church has to face suffering"). What is more striking, though, is that the pope's words evoke Raymond's own characterization of Catherine as a weak woman. Is Raymond here seeking papal approval of his own assessment of the saint?

This episode is followed by a further request from Pope Urban that Catherine, together with Catherine of Sweden, should visit the Queen of Naples to dissuade her from supporting the schismatics. Without consulting Catherine, Raymond tells the pope this is a bad idea and would harm the women's reputations, though Catherine of Sweden had in any case declined to travel. Raymond is duly rebuked by Catherine for his intervention. We are then told that Pope Urban wanted to send Raymond to France to try to persuade the French king to dissociate himself from the schism. Catherine advises him to do as the pope wishes:

> Take it as certain, Father, that whatever the schismatics falsely claim, he [Urban] is indeed the genuine Vicar of Christ. It is my will that you should preach and defend the truth of this, as you would that of the Catholic faith itself.[34]

Raymond departs and records that this is the last time he saw Catherine alive.

---

[33] Ibid., p. 311.

[34] Ibid., p. 313.

While, then, Catherine clearly advocates the cause of the Roman papacy, Raymond's treatment of this episode—as a go-between for Catherine and the pope, and as expressing a view that she does not endorse—appears to be an exercise in enhancing his own reputation as well.

Asserting a male presence

Women mystics are not always kindly received by other women. Fra Giunta recounts an episode in the life of Margaret of Cortona in which he describes local women coming "with great devotion" to watch Margaret at prayer.[35] One of Margaret's companions, thinking to act in the saint's best interests, tries to shoo them away using words that were "not well chosen", which provokes a loud and unseemly argument with one particular woman, that even the intervention of Margaret herself could not silence. Fra Giunta's comment is that "a ruffled temper, especially in a woman, sees an insult even in what is well-meant".

The power of women's words is noted on another occasion when Margaret reproves one of her helpers for seeking gifts for herself and her children rather than just for the community: "the woman got angry and loudly denied what she had done, and with many cutting words insulted Margaret."[36] Whether a man would have been described in those terms is a matter of conjecture, but in this instance Fra Giunta refrains from further comment.

Nonetheless, biographers' comments on the perceived nature of women, and the representation of their behaviour, are significant in this context, since they represent an assertion of male presence. Readers are not allowed to forget that although the subject is a woman, it is thanks to a man that her story is recounted.

Agnes
The shorter format of Raymond of Capua's first biography offers little scope for the biographer to express his opinions. Raymond does, however, like

---

35   Fr Cuthbert, *A Tuscan Penitent*, p. 82.

36   Ibid., p. 85.

those who recorded the legends of Syriac women saints long before him, appeal to male witnesses to lend weight to specific aspects of Agnes' story.

An early miracle associated with Agnes concerns a meal at which she joins visitors to her monastery and a rose appears where she is seated (see p. 185 above). However, it is the visitors who are particularly significant here: "men of great penitential austerity ... men of praiseworthy reputation and high sanctity, whose way of life was to dwell in solitude and give themselves up wholly to contemplation of the Creator."[37] This gives rise to "a pious dispute" as to whether the rose is a sign of Agnes' holiness or whether it is in celebration of their fellowship, a dispute where "each won the victory and even fuller concord reigned than at first". So while the holy men are present to attest to the miraculous revelation of Agnes' sanctity, there is no loss of face, not least because of Agnes' holy humility in seeking an alternative explanation.

Similarly, the diocesan bishop and attendant cleric are witnesses when the church where Agnes is to receive the veil is filled with manna from heaven, a phenomenon already witnessed by her sisters whenever Agnes rose from her prayers. The Church authorities are cited to give added credence to the presence of the "minute manna, like snow", to which Raymond comments that it is a miracle "which I do not recall having read about any other man or woman".[38]

Witnesses are, of course, always important, and in his Prologue, Raymond notes that there have been "many men and women witnesses", who have since died. Few, however, appear in the biography, although when possible Raymond is at pains to indicate the presence of men. There is, for example, "the male superior of the monastery" who entrusts the fourteen-year-old Agnes with the job of cellarer (that is, being in charge of provisions), in recognition of her "prudence and agreeable . . . arrangement of all her behaviour".[39]

---

[37] Ibid., p. 48.

[38] Ibid., pp. 22, 23.

[39] Ibid., p. 14.

Biographical omissions

"Inglese italianato è un diavolo incarnate" (an Italianized Englishman is a devil incarnate).[40]

Unsurprisingly, Raymond of Capua is silent on Catherine's dealings with an infamous English mercenary who was particularly active in Florence and northern Italy in the 1370s. This may be out of concern for his own reputation as well as for hers, since they both appear to have been associated with an alleged plot, probably inspired by the papacy, to destabilize Siena. Indeed, Raymond's own brother Luigi, whom Catherine would get released from prison in 1377, was also a mercenary and would, a decade after Catherine's death, fight alongside the Englishman.

Not a lot is known about John Hawkwood (dubbed, in an Italian play on words, Giovanni Acuto—John the sharp one), who hailed from a well-connected family in Essex and became a career mercenary. He fought at Crécy in 1346 and at Poitiers ten years later, and during the 1360s was involved in attacks on Avignon when the popes were in residence there. Thereafter, Hawkwood switched sides several times, engaging in raids and extortion either on behalf of the pope or of his enemies.

It seems that Catherine's contact with this rather unsavoury character came about through her commitment to bringing the Avignon papacy back to Rome. Clearly Catherine lacked the regal authority of Bridget of Sweden, who had been in a position to tell Urban V that he would die if he abandoned Rome for Avignon (a prophecy that was duly fulfilled). Instead, Catherine gets drawn in through her political support, and that of some of her followers, for the Salimbeni family, who had controlled the government of Siena until 1371, and whom the pope was keen to see reinstated in his pursuit of stability. According to Stonor Saunders' research, Raymond was an accomplice of the Salimbeni in Montepulciano and was not averse to using his position as Catherine's confessor to pursue

---

[40]   A saying said to have been inspired by the activities of John Hawkwood; see Frances Stonor Saunders, *Hawkwood: Diabolical Englishman* (London: Faber and Faber, 2004), p. xvii.

his own ends, which included seeking the support of Hawkwood and his company.[41]

In 1375, Raymond met with John Hawkwood, on the pretext of delivering a letter to him from Catherine. In it she urged the Englishman to change direction and set out on a crusade to the Holy Land. This could have been an excuse they dreamt up between them, that would allow Raymond access to Hawkwood's camp. Or it may have been an attempt to win support for a project that was close to the heart of the absent Pope Gregory XI. Or possibly both. In her letter Catherine writes:

> You find so much satisfaction in fighting and waging war, so now I am begging you tenderly in Christ Jesus not to wage war any longer against Christians (for that offends God), but to go instead to fight the unbelievers, as God and our holy father have decreed.[42]

Most probably, Catherine understood that she could put the pope's involvement with a frankly cruel and unprincipled mercenary to better use, if Hawkwood could be persuaded to undertake a crusade instead. Inevitably this was doomed to fail. So, unlike St Bridget, Catherine's lack of social standing could instead have led her to be associated with political scheming and with an unscrupulous military leader, both of which might have tarnished her and Raymond's reputation. Raymond's silence on the matter in his life of Catherine leaves the mystery unresolved but preserves the picture of the saint that he is intent on constructing.

There are, however, several details from all this that Raymond does include, although he removes from them any suggestion of political collusion on Catherine's part. One is a reference to a healing miracle for a woman "possessed by a devil", whom Catherine cures at the request of one Donna Biachina, "widow of a certain Giovanni Angelini dei Salimbeni"

---

[41]   Stonor Saunders' book offers a thorough account of the historical and political background to Hawkwood's undertakings, although inevitably a shortage of evidence regarding Hawkwood's association with Raymond and Catherine means that details of their story remain at the level of conjecture.

[42]   Quoted in *Hawkwood: Diabolical Englishman*, p. 187.

with whom she and Raymond had been staying. Raymond adds that he himself was not present at the time, "for Catherine had sent me just then on certain Church affairs to the Vicar of Christ, his Lordship Pope Gregory XI".[43] Maybe Raymond was trying to distance himself from the Salimbeni, or maybe he just wished to stress his own importance. Either way, Raymond adds a forceful conclusion:

> [These things] have been written that the Reader may realise for himself how powerful a charism of exorcising evil spirits Catherine had received from heaven. It was fitting that she should, for she had already, the grace of Christ accompanying, fought a mighty campaign against them in their wickedness and won an overwhelming victory over them.[44]

One episode in Catherine's life that Raymond does not mention is also one of the best-known. It is the story of Nicolò di Toldo, a young aristocrat who was executed in 1375, apparently for offending the Sienese rulers. Catherine herself describes her involvement in comforting the young man, in a letter to Raymond. A possible explanation for this oversight is that this infamous "letter 273" may not be genuine and scholarly opinion remains divided. Perhaps Raymond simply considered that the image of Catherine cradling a severed head was unseemly and a poor fit with the picture of the saint he was aiming to convey.

In Catherine's description of events, it seems that she converted the young man, hearing his confession and taking him to Mass, where he received Communion for the first time. If that is the case, bearing in mind that a close bond is not unusual between a person who has come to faith and the one who has converted them, it is perhaps not so surprising that Catherine speaks of Nicolò in the kind of sensuous language that she might otherwise use of Christ himself. On the day of the execution, Catherine, who had already laid her own head on the block, becomes rapt in prayer. And, in what was no doubt the cause of scandal, she caressed his head both before and after his execution, as she wrote to Raymond: "I

---

43   *Life of St Catherine of Siena*, p. 255.

44   Ibid., p. 257.

have just received a Head in my hands, which was to me of such sweetness as heart cannot think, nor tongue say, nor eye see, nor the ears hear."[45]

However, in an extraordinary appropriation of the saint and her story, the British poet Alice Meynell's 1921 poem "Saint Catherine of Siena" ends with a plea for modern man to show the same respect for a woman as did the penitent criminal, that is via universal suffrage, since Meynell was committed to the Suffragettes' cause. The final stanzas read as follows:

> Death. He did fear it, in his cell,
> Darkling amid the Tuscan sun;
> And, weeping, at her feet he fell,
> The sacred, young, provincial nun.
>
> She prayed, she preached him innocent;
> She gave him to the Sacrificed;
> On her courageous breast he leant,
> The breast where beat the heart of Christ.
>
> He left it for the block, with cries
> Of victory on his severed breath.
> That crimson head she clasped, her eyes
> Blind with the splendour of his death.
>
> And will the man of modern years
> —Stern on the Vote—withhold from thee,
> Thou prop, thou cross, erect, in tears,
> Catherine, the service of his knee?

In referring to other examples of omission, Raymond pleads negligence or simple forgetfulness, particularly when it comes to "favours" associated with Catherine after her death, which may well have lived on in popular memory:

---

45 Vida D. Scudder (tr. and ed.), *Saint Catherine of Siena as seen in her letters*, p. 51, available at <https://www.gutenberg.org/ebooks/7403>, accessed 25 September 2021.

I acknowledge myself guilty in this: that many people, both men and women, came to me with accounts of wonderful favours which they had received through Catherine's merits, and I, through negligence on my own part rather than on the part of others, allowed the faces to be buried in oblivion. I was not diligent enough in noting them down in writing. I did, however, at one time employ a notary specially to do this; but he too was negligent about recording them.[46]

He also adds that while he may have received accounts of various favours, "my memory is failing with advancing years, and I can no longer remember all the others in detail", an excuse, perhaps, for curtailing a book that "has already dragged on in such protracted fashion".[47]

---

[46]   *Life of St Catherine of Siena*, p. 358.

[47]   Ibid., p. 359.

CHAPTER 10

Holy women and the Church

Just as biographers have a multi-faceted role in giving an account of their subjects—pleading for them to be recognized as holy while at the same time promoting certain interests of their own—so too the Church's role is far from straightforward. Attitudes ranged from wanting to keep in check women who were regarded as dangerous to using them for the Church's own ends. Similarly, holy women themselves needed to be presented as conforming to the Church's teaching, without their own special gifts being compromised. With the passage of time, some elements of mystical experience came to be accepted into Catholic liturgies, and a few of the canonization processes eventually reached a conclusion.

Arguing for canonization

The life stories of holy men and women were a crucial part of the canonization process.[1] Lombardelli's closely structured narratives set out a clear pattern of such accounts, while other biographies vary in the extent to which the writers' desire to see their subject canonized is made explicit. Even so, the episodes they recount and the language they use are carefully chosen to make a case. Typically this is reflected in a desire to emphasize the orthodoxy of the holy woman's practices, however far removed from the mainstream they may appear to be. Appeals to

---

[1] An exception is Tommaso da Celano's biography of Clare of Assisi, who was canonized in 1255. Tommaso's final chapter simply notes the fact of canonization, having previously noted relatively few miracles ascribed to the saint after her death.

respected witnesses, and the close association with monastic Orders as already described are all part of this process.

The medieval canonization process depended above all on the testimony of local people and the gathering of information by a local priest, who then produced a *Legenda*. This served both an educational purpose—to inspire the faithful along a similar path of holiness—and a practical one, which was to make an official case for sainthood. Naturally, when seeking recognition of their own saint, local people responded enthusiastically, with many accounts of miracles recorded after the saint's death. But they rarely waited for due process to run its course. Angela of Foligno was referred to in the region as St Angela long before her relatively recent canonization.

This could, however, be a risky process, if the would-be saint was regarded by some groups as heretical. This was arguably a hindrance to the canonization of Clare of Montefalco, whose *processo* took place in 1318-19. Despite her active opposition to the Free Spirit heresy, she was in the minds of some too closely associated with it for comfort. As Goodrich comments, "The power of a saint rested upon his conformity to a tradition of sainthood accepted by the community he served."[2] Another drawback was Clare's claim to "internal" stigmatization at a time when the Church had doubts as to whether such a phenomenon existed.

Agnes

In Raymond of Capua's life of Agnes of Montepulciano, the aim of canonization is rarely made explicit. The exception comes early on, when a respected nun is sent by the bishop to visit Agnes' monastery. This woman prophesies of Agnes that, just like the martyr St Agnes of Rome, "this holy girl will second the same name within the Church Militant", a prophecy which Raymond claims has been fulfilled even though Agnes

---

[2]   Michael Goodrich, "The politics of canonization in the thirteenth century: lay and mendicant saints", in S. Wilson (ed.), *Saints and Their Cults: Studies in Religious Sociology, Folklore and History* (Cambridge: Cambridge University Press, 1983), pp. 169–87, here at p. 176.

"has not been enrolled by the Supreme Pontiff in the catalogue of saints" despite "the abundant evidence of miracles" attributed to her.[3]

Raymond then appears to lose patience with the pontiff:

> I do not know what the Pope wants, because all the people call both the monastery and the church by the name of "St. Agnes". In this I see nothing except that the Lord who is faithful in all his words, having made this promise prophetically through his handmaid, will fulfil it presently in deed . . . And I hope that, as a perfect and unfailing artist, he will fulfil more perfectly what he has said, when he will plainly adorn with honor and praise his saint now exalted in the Church Triumphant, by numbering her among the society of holy virgins in the Church Militant through the agency of his vicar, the successor of Peter.[4]

In this way, Raymond establishes the premise of his whole account: Agnes is already among the saints in heaven, but, like Margaret of Cortona before her, she lacks the endorsement of the Church on earth.

As previously indicated (Chapter 3 above), Raymond is at pains to stress Agnes' conformity, illustrating her obedience both to her initial Augustinian Order and to the diocesan bishop in seeking permission to build her church and describing her as "someone entirely Catholic". His comment is all the more heartfelt as he goes on to recount the handing over of that church to the Dominicans:

> After a certain space of time, first from the bishop then from the legate of the Apostolic See, she obtained . . . that the care of this monastery be committed to the Order of Friars Preachers . . . Thus the Supreme Shepherd might show clearly through his vicars that the work of Agnes was acceptable in the sight of his majesty.[5]

---

3   *Life of St Agnes of Montepulciano*, p. 11.

4   Ibid., p. 12.

5   Ibid., pp. 60–1.

When Raymond comes to write his biography of Catherine of Siena, he is still arguing for recognition of Agnes. Catherine was keen to visit Agnes' relics after she had a vision which revealed to her that "in the Kingdom of Heaven she was to be put on a level with the blessed Sister Agnes of Montepulciano, and was to have her as a companion in everlasting bliss".[6] Before alluding to the miracles associated with Agnes after her death, Raymond notes that "this Sister, though her name has not yet been inscribed in the catalogue of the Saints, had the way to sainthood prepared before her by the many graces she was blessed with by the loving-kindness of God".[7] The implication is clear: to accept the sanctity of the one is to accept also the sanctity of the other.

Catherine of Siena

Raymond's long biography of Catherine of Siena ends with a summary of her life and a direct plea for canonization: "From all that has been written in this work the final conclusion to be drawn is: that it is a fitting thing that this holy Virgin and Martyr should be enrolled by the Church Militant in the catalogue of the Saints."[8] While his *Life* contains all the general elements long thought necessary to establish sanctity, depicting, for example, the saint constantly withstanding temptation and working miracles after death, Raymond also inserts references to Catherine's holiness throughout the book. As with his treatment of Agnes, he refers to popular acclaim,[9] but his preferred technique seems to lie in establishing comparisons with saints already in the canon.

Early in his work Raymond includes a long digression on what he calls "the infinite variety of individual types of sanctity".[10] So he invokes the *Lives* of the Desert Fathers, such as Hilarion, Macarius and Arsenius who, he claims, had the advantage of being guided by distinguished teachers and the discipline of a monastic Order. By contrast, Catherine had to

---

6   *Life of St Catherine of Siena*, p. 299.

7   Ibid., p. 300.

8   Ibid., p. 388.

9   "Catherine's fame for sanctity now began to spread far and wide amongst the people, and to shine ever brighter day by day", ibid., p. 154.

10   Ibid., p. 60.

manage in her own home, was obstructed by her family and had no one to guide her, yet "she reached, in this matter of abstinence from food, a height of perfection which none of those mentioned could attain to".[11] Nonetheless, he is at pains to point out that he is not trying to rank her above those earlier saints, although the implication is that she is at least equal to them.

Raymond later returns to the theme of Catherine's abstinence and comparison with the Fathers and other saints, only to protest that "the degree of a person's holiness is judged and measured, not by the measure of his fasting, but by the measure of his charity".[12] He also resumes his argument about "singularity" of holiness, which, in the case of Catherine's extreme fasting, is understood by Catherine herself as God-given: "Because of my sins, God has let me fall victim to a singular kind of weakness or defect, which makes it quite impossible for me to take food."[13]

Perhaps the most effective plea for Catherine's sanctity, however, lies not in Raymond's arguments but in his account of a vision given to one of Catherine's early critics, an elderly invalid called Andrea. As she lies in bed and Catherine comes in to nurse her, Andrea has a vision of transfiguration, as she sees:

> . . . a flood of light pouring down from above, and bathing the whole bed with a radiance so serene and so soothing that it charmed away from her all sense of pain. As her eyes darted about . . . to discover the source of this unearthly radiance, she became aware that it had suffused the features of her nurse also, transfiguring the face of the one she knew as Catherine the daughter of Lapa into that of a majestic angel, and mantling her whole body, too, with refulgent splendour.[14]

Thereafter Andrea insists that Catherine was a saint, referring to her experience of seeing "Catherine transfigured before her and bathed in

---

[11] Ibid., p. 59.

[12] Ibid., p. 167.

[13] Ibid., p. 168.

[14] Ibid., p. 153.

the light of heaven".[15] The unmistakable scriptural reference, along with Raymond's use of a witness who was formerly biased against Catherine, is a powerful addition to his arguments for canonization.

Christ's promise to Margaret of Cortona

Despite being acclaimed as a saint from the day of her death by local people, who built a church to honour her, Margaret of Cortona was not canonized until 1728. Fra Giunta's account of her life does not openly advocate for canonization. Instead, he reports words spoken to her by Christ in a vision, which suggest that a place among the elect is hers for the asking:

> The Lord showed her the blessed Francis, together with a multitude of Saints, and He asked her why she did not desire their companionship. And Margaret replied, "Lord, I desire the company of the Saints, yea, and of all the heavenly court; but it is to Thee my soul adheres with constant yearning . . .". The Lord replied: "My child, since thou dost seek Me alone I will make thee great in the mansions of My glory, and there thou shalt possess Me in great gladness."[16]

When Margaret died, this promise appeared to be fulfilled, according to the witness of "a certain eminent soul" who had a vision of Margaret going up to heaven without first passing through Purgatory:

> His spirit beheld the spirit of Margaret, beaming with ineffable joy, taken up into heaven, together with a multitude of souls newly released from purgatory. And from that day this person spoke of Margaret as Christ's second Magdalene.[17]

Attentive readers of Fra Giunta's account will have noted that he has already reported Margaret's vision of Mary Magdalene, who is described

---

[15]   Ibid., p. 54.

[16]   Fr Cuthbert, *A Tuscan Penitent*, p. 68.

[17]   Ibid., p. 124.

as "Magdalene the Blessed, most faithful of Christ's apostles, clothed in a robe as it were of silver and crowned with a crown of precious gems and surrounded by the holy angels".[18] As the story of the "second Magdelene", Margaret's *Legenda* appears to endorse popular views as to her sanctity, not by personal opinion or conventional witnesses, but through the most holy of intermediaries.

Michael Goodrich has effectively exposed some of the political forces behind canonizations, demonstrating how the Church was able to use holy men and women, particularly laypeople, for its own ends.[19] Thus the canonization process brought together, on the one hand, the saints' own piety and good works, and, on the other, the immediate needs of the Church, whether that lay in the fight against heresy or the influence of powerful families or dynasties.[20] Goodrich concludes:

> While the Christian idealism and *imitatio Christi* embodied in the life of the saint remained paramount, the immediate aims behind papally confirmed sainthood were specific, and limited by the political interests of Rome.[21]

Promoting doctrine

The biographer's role in defending the Church from heresy, by insisting on his subject's orthodoxy, is balanced by a certain concern to promote innovation. The new feasts of the Sacred Heart and the Five Wounds of Jesus take their expression from the mystics' devotion to the Passion of Christ, while doctrines are explicitly formulated. Thus the biographer of Clare of Montefalco selects visions that relate specifically to the concerns

---

[18] Ibid., p. 93.

[19] Goodrich, "The politics of canonization in the thirteenth century", n. 2 above, especially pp. 170–9.

[20] These external influences are far from being a thing of the past: consider the delay in canonizing the twentieth-century saint Oscar Romero, attributed to the powerful families of El Salvador.

[21] N. 2 above, p. 183.

of the contemporary Church. They include reverence for the Eucharist (*pace* Free Spirit heretics), and for the practices of extreme unction and penance, which were being misused in that they were often carried out by non-priests.

Klotz notes that the words attributed to Clare in a conversation with Marina on the Eucharist and the Real Presence of Christ closely follow the words of Lateran IV:

> In a certain vision, the Lord revealed to me how the substance of the bread and wine in the blink of an eye at the words said by the presbyter immediately are changed in substance into the Body and Blood of Christ.[22]

In 1274, the doctrine of Purgatory had been set out by the Second Council of Lyon, which stated that in the case of people who had repented of their sins before death but who had not done suitable penance for them, "their souls are cleansed after death by purgatorial or purifying punishments". Those punishments could be relieved by the "offerings of the living faithful".[23]

Thirty years later, Fra Giunta records the Lord's words to Margaret of Cortona:

> Tell the Friars Minor that they ever bear in mind the souls of the dead who suffer for their sins in purgatory, for they are a vast multitude beyond the thought of man, and they are helped but little by those on earth, even by those who are dear to them; and tell the Friars also that those of them who occupy themselves with worldly affairs will have much to suffer in purgatory.[24]

---

[22] Sister Margaret Elizabeth Klotz, OSF, *Clare of Montefalco (1268–1308): The life of the soul is the love of God* (PhD thesis, University of St Michael's College, Toronto, 2001), pp. 147, 148–9.

[23] *De sorte defunctorum.*

[24] Fr Cuthbert, *A Tuscan Penitent*, p. 111.

This undisguised appeal to the Order to be faithful in their prayers for the dead as well as to look to their own behaviour is presumably an issue close to the heart of Margaret's biographer.

The doctrine of Purgatory remained contentious. It was upheld at the Council of Florence and the Council of Trent but condemned by Martin Luther and his followers. The fifteenth-century mystic Catherine of Genoa would write her own *Treatise on Purgatory* (see General Conclusion below).

In her thesis on Clare of Montefalco, Klotz observes that "Clare lived out and brought forward the teachings of the Church on Purgatory, especially those stressing the expiatory aid of prayer in shortening the soul's punishment",[25] a further detail that would have been helpful in the building of Clare's reputation for orthodoxy.

In the case of Catherine of Siena, however, no further argumentation is needed. In one of her most profound ecstatic experiences Catherine saw Purgatory for herself: "I saw the punishments undergone both by the damned and by the souls in Purgatory, and these likewise no words can adequately describe."[26] Indeed, the assumption to be drawn from Raymond's work is that the doctrine is not in dispute. By her prayers, Catherine freed criminals from Purgatory, and in particular she prayed that her God-fearing father might be spared the pains of Purgatory. Catherine's prayer, however, is answered at a cost: as Giacomo died, she felt a stabbing pain in her side that would never leave her. In return, Catherine is able to see what happened to him after death: "she [saw] that soul, as it left the darkness of the body here below, enter straight away into perpetual light."[27]

---

[25] Klotz, *Clare of Montefalco*, p. 113.

[26] *Life of St Catherine of Siena*, p. 204.

[27] Ibid., p. 211.

Devotional practices

The Five Wounds and the Sacred Heart

The female mystics' special focus on the suffering of Christ has had several lasting effects on the devotional practice of the Church. The Feast of the Sacred Heart of Jesus dates only from the mid-nineteenth century, when it was instituted as a holy day of obligation by Pope Pius IX, to be observed on the third Friday after Pentecost. Its origins, however, lie firmly in medieval practice; Christ's physical heart is seen as representing his love for the world, a love which is also represented by devotion to the wounds of Christ in his hands, feet and side. This leads to the pain of the wounds being felt in the mystics' own bodies.

Margaret of Cortona's near constant inner turmoil stems from her steadfast refusal to accept that she has been forgiven, despite Christ's repeated assurances to the contrary. In response, the Lord is said to "take Margaret's part against herself": "know for a certainty that from the sole of thy foot to the crown of thy head I have crowned thee with grace and adorned thee with virtue." He then offers her his Five Wounds as a weapon in this inner battle: "take to thyself My Five Wounds to be thy weapons against the enemy." Whereupon Margaret, "contemplating the wound in his side, said: 'Lord, grant me a full understanding of Thy goodness and a perfect love of Thee.'"[28] Thus the most severe of Christ's wounds becomes a further symbol of his love, and devotion to the marks of his suffering for the sins of the world becomes an unassailable protection in times of spiritual conflict.

Devotion to the Sacred Heart arises from the conviction that, on the cross, the soldier's spear penetrated Jesus' heart as well as his side. Raymond of Capua relays Catherine's description:

> She used to add ... that she experienced in her own poor body some little share of each single suffering of our Lord; but as for sharing any one of them in its totality, that she deemed impossible. Another thing she used to say was that the greatest pain our Saviour suffered on the Cross was that in his breast,

---

[28]   Fr Cuthbert, *A Tuscan Penitent*, pp. 73–4.

on account of the dislocation of the bones of his chest. As an
indication that this must have been so, she used to say that in
her own aching body the other pains would pass, and only that
in the breast would remain on always . . . she said this other pain
remained always more excruciating.[29]

Raymond adds his own endorsement: "I can easily imagine how this was
so, both for her and for our Lord and Saviour himself, on account of the
heart lying close alongside."[30] He goes on to recount how this sharing in
Christ's Passion led to Catherine's physical decline, until her own heart
was rent in two, when thanks to the "sheer intensity of her love for God"
she breathed her last.

Catherine's experience of pain is externalized in her report of a vision
in which Jesus physically replaces her own heart with one that is "ruby
in colour and ablaze with light", leaving a scar in her flesh as a tangible
sign of this miracle.[31]

Like the stigmata, the physical appearance of suffering in the form
of Christ's heart was taken up in art, as artists sought to make real an
intrinsically hidden mystical experience. In Sienese art, Catherine is
represented as exchanging hearts with her Lord. Guidoccio Cozzarelli
(1450–1517) shows Catherine kneeling before an altar, holding a heart
which she is either giving to or receiving from the figure of Christ who is
stretching out to her from what appears to be an artwork above the altar.

Francesco Vanni, on the other hand, whose pictures of the saint and her
Saviour are notable for their erotic overtones, depicts Catherine leaning
close into Christ, a heart in her left hand, as she gazes adoringly into his face.

Devotion to the Sacred Heart spread across much of Europe from
the fourteenth century onwards, being reflected, for example, in the
Dominican rosary, but it has never become a feast day for the whole
Church. Whether this might change with Pope Francis and his own
devotion to Christ's wounds (which in 2018 he admitted "may sound a
bit medieval") remains to be seen.

---

[29]   *Life of St Catherine of Siena*, p. 201.

[30]   Ibid.

[31]   Ibid., p. 175.

Stigmata

The longing of medieval mystics for complete oneness with Christ, their devotion to his Passion, and their concern especially to reflect on his physical wounds, resulted in their taking on his suffering for themselves. In describing Clare of Montefalco's self-identification with the "crucified humanity of Jesus", Klotz is careful to set the saint's physical suffering in the context of her whole Christian life: "Clare suffered both internal and external pains in direct imitation of Christ's suffering. But this . . . also placed her in direct contact with the internal and external sufferings of others."[32] In other words, Clare's compassion for Jesus' suffering enabled her to show greater compassion for the suffering of others.

Besides the wounds in Christ's hands, feet and side, contemplation of the effects of scourging and the pain of the crown of thorns was also a means of sharing his suffering. And for some, this devotion to Christ's Passion led quite naturally to feeling the pain of his wounds in their own bodies and, occasionally, to displaying outward signs of it as well. Furthermore, the appearance of stigmata on the hands and feet of St Francis, together with the discovery, after death, that Clare of Montefalco's body contained miniature replicas of the instruments of the Passion, attracted the attention of the Church and took the understanding of sharing in Christ's suffering to a whole new level.

Fra Giunta's description of Margaret's very public manifestation of suffering with Christ refers to the "marks of suffering" that appeared in her, but these, though, are the signs of death rather than the wounds of crucifixion: "She clenched her teeth, her face became discoloured and her pulse ceased to beat. She was unable to speak and became quite cold."[33]

The debates around whether it was possible for a woman, following the example of Francis, to receive the stigmata would preoccupy the Church for many years, from the thirteenth century onwards. It was known that St Clare of Assisi, around the time that Francis received the stigmata, contracted an illness from which she never recovered. This was accepted as a suitable sign of her union with the suffering Christ, without the

---

[32]   Klotz, *Clare of Montefalco*, p. 180.

[33]   Fr Cuthbert, *A Tuscan Penitent*, p. 78.

need for outward symbolism. It is sometimes claimed that Angela of Foligno may have received the stigmata, though only temporarily. This is not mentioned by Arnaldo, but if correct, the rumours may well have hampered any claim to canonization.

Clearly recognizable wounds were for most lay Christians an incontrovertible sign of holiness. Rather like the physical reality of relics, and their association with miraculous healing, the stigmata in particular were all the concrete evidence they needed to be convinced of the special nature of their own saint. Suffering with Christ could now be clearly visualized and popularized by artists who depicted dramatic scenes of receiving the stigmata, or who routinely included wounded hands and feet in their portrayals of Francis, Catherine of Siena and others.

Raymond of Capua's account of Catherine receiving the stigmata does, however, acknowledge that there is a problem with so-called "invisible" stigmata, and he addresses this by describing her stigmatization as taking place in two stages. In the first instance, Catherine's confessor Fra Tommaso is an integral part of the narrative: while Catherine was praying for him specifically, she had asked for a pledge that her prayer had been answered. Tommaso subsequently asked Catherine to describe her vision, and receives this account:

> I said, "What token will you give me, Lord, as a pledge that you will do this for me?" "Stretch out your hand to me", he replied. I did so. He took a nail, rested the point of it on the centre of the palm of my hand, and pressed it into my hand with such force that it seemed to pierce right through it, and I felt agony as if an iron nail had been driven through it with a hammer. So now, Father, by the grace of my Lord Jesus Christ, I bear this stigma in my right hand; and though others cannot see it, its reality is testified to myself by the evidence of my senses and by the pain it gives me, which never ceases.[34]

On the second occasion, much later, Raymond himself witnessed Catherine's ecstatic vision. He tells us that while she was in ecstasy he took

---

[34]   *Life of St Catherine of Siena*, p. 185.

"careful note of the attitudes and movements of her body, endeavouring to fathom their significance", and he asks her to tell him what had happened:

> I saw our Lord, fastened to the cross, coming down upon me in a blaze of light . . . Then I saw, springing from the marks of his most sacred wounds, five blood-red rays coming down upon me, directed towards my hands and feet and heart. Realising the meaning of the mystery, I promptly cried out: "Ah, Lord, my God, I implore you not to let the marks show outwardly on my body."[35]

In response to Raymond's questions about her pain, she replied: "So intense is the pain I feel in those five parts, and especially in my heart, that I believe that nothing but a further miracle of our Lord will make it possible for this body to survive such suffering." And indeed, Raymond goes on to witness and record evidence of Catherine's physical pain.

While Catherine's account may well have been influenced by popular representations of the stigmatization of St Francis, Raymond uses his familiar narrative device of reliable witnesses to demonstrate the reality of the visions and the pain caused by them in order to argue for the genuine existence of invisible stigmata. As already noted (see Chapter 5), Catherine was not officially recognized as a stigmatic for more than two centuries after her death. During this time unseemly arguments raged between the Dominicans and the Franciscans about the validity of her stigmata, culminating in Lombardelli's *Sommario*,[36] commissioned by Pope Clement VIII in the hope of bringing the dispute to an end. During this interim period, the question of stigmata received considerable publicity, thanks not least to Pope Sixtus IV, who forbade artists from depicting stigmata in their portrayal of Catherine. Although this might have hindered the process of recognition,[37] it could only heighten the

---

[35] Ibid., p. 186.

[36] *Sommario della disputa a difesa delle Sacre Stimate di Santa Caterina da Siena* (Siena, 1601).

[37] For a full account of this process, see Carolyn Muessig, *The Stigmata in Medieval and Early Modern Europe* (Oxford: Oxford University Press, 2020), pp. 183–8.

awareness of the disputed stigmata on the part of the faithful. As Muessig comments:

> Ultimately, the strong Dominican initiative to have Catherine of Siena recognized as a stigmatic saint also established a strong theological position regarding the appropriateness for women to be bearers of the holy wounds.[38]

So it was that the Church, along with artists and Dominican apologists, had a part to play in enabling a particular conceptualization of Catherine to predominate, as well as setting a pattern for the recognition of other stigmatics who emerged subsequently.

Serving the interests of Church and state: Gregorio Lombardelli

> [The] ability to unify a particular region or class around the banner of one or another charismatic figure was a potent force through which the papacy successfully maintained the unity and universality of a beleaguered faith.[39]

In the mid-sixteenth century, catastrophe struck Siena. With the support of Emperor Charles V, Cosmo de' Medici set out to conquer Florence's last remaining rival in Tuscany, the Republic of Siena. In 1555, the republic, allied to France, surrendered to Spain, and in 1559 it was incorporated into the Duchy of Florence. Thereafter, the Grand Duchy of Tuscany would be ruled by the Medici family for the best part of 200 years.

When, therefore, in the 1580s, Gregorio Lombardelli wrote a series of *Lives* of lesser-known Sienese holy men and women from earlier times, most of them Dominicans, it is hard not to see his work as a claim to moral superiority of his home state and his own Order, with his work

---

38 Ibid., p. 188.
39 Goodrich, "The politics of canonization in the thirteenth century", p. 170.

on the defence of the stigmata of Catherine of Siena (1601) providing a further boost to the reputation of both.

Lombardelli's biographies all follow a straightforward chronological pattern, beginning with details of the subjects' family background and ending with their death and any miracles subsequently associated with them. Among the features that are common to all of them, women and men alike, Lombardelli highlights in particular their temptations and engagement with the Devil. The *Vita* of Beata Nera Tolomei (1583)[40] describes the Devil's activities in her early life, not only in tempting her to succumb to lust, but also in causing her mother and a servant to try to obstruct her vocation. The Devil gets his comeuppance when a young man whom the Devil has caused to fall in love with her is instead converted by Nera, which brings his interference to an end. By contrast, the 1584 *Vita* of Beato Gio Batista Tolomei, who was converted by Beata Nera, shows him as being beset by temptation throughout his life as a Dominican.

Four of Lombardelli's lives—of Aldobrandesca, Genovese of Siena (1586), about whom little is known, Nera Tolomei and Gio Batista Tolomei—record a degree of overlap between them. The closest relationship, unsurprisingly, is between the two members of the Tolomei family. Gio Batista has a dream where Nera convinces him to remain in the Dominican Order; after Nera's death, Gio Batista, finding himself in a life-threatening situation, prays to her, asking that just as she saved him from the Devil, she would save him and his companion from drowning. Later, Gio Batista is present at Aldobrandesca's death and comforts her.

There is, too, a bond between Beata Nera and Genovese. After the death of her parents and husband, Genovese is consoled by Beata Nera, which leads to her also becoming a Third Order Dominican. At the end of her life, Genovese is told by Nera when she will die. Interestingly, though, when Genovese is reported as withstanding temptation by the Devil to abandon her good works, it is to God and her "advocate" Catherine that Genovese turns in thanksgiving.

---

[40]   B. Nera was a Third Order Dominican, whom Lombardelli presents as "noblissima Sanese" (a most noble Sienese).

Taken individually, Lombardelli's *Lives* are worthy but unremarkable. Together, though, they create a picture of holiness associated with a specific place and time in history. Together, they also give us a composite ideal of a holy woman: one who is given to good works and ascetic practices; one who has to some degree gifts of prophecy and of miraculous healing; and who perhaps above all can withstand all that the tempter throws at her. If Lombardelli's prime motivation was to promote both his Order and his native Siena, he has done so in a way that transcends individual detail and conjures up a general aura of holiness surrounding his compatriots of a former age.

William of Flete's memorial sermon for Catherine

> Alas for the Church of God, that it did not listen to her advice, that is, to the advice of the Lord; alas for the Church of God which has lost so great a light! Alas for us who have lost so good a mother, who carried our sins and those of the Church in her heart through many crosses![41]

William of Flete composed his sermon for the second anniversary of Catherine's death. It is unclear whether it was intended to be delivered or, given its length, simply meant to be read. Like countless eulogies recited at funerals today, it contains biographical detail and pays tribute to the qualities of the deceased, although its overall purpose is a far cry from "the deceased and me" theme that is popular in today's churches and crematoria.

Memorial sermons of the past had some quite specific functions. They were intended to console the living while commending the deceased; they could be used to encourage people to pray for the dead, and to reflect on death generally; they expressed collective grief and lamentation, as

---

[41] "Remembering Catherine", in B. Hackett, O.S.A., *William Flete, O.S.A., and Catherine of Siena* (Villanova, PA: Augustinian Press, 1992), pp. 185–221, here at p. 198.

William does above.[42] And, of course, then, as now, they were designed to show the deceased person in the best possible light. William's sermon does all that, but, more importantly, while also roaming freely across the events of Catherine's life it demonstrates that William intends us to remember Catherine in a very specific way and encourages us to draw from that a manifesto for the future.

Throughout William's sermon, Catherine is inseparable from "the Church of God". It is for the good of the Church that Catherine has suffered in various ways, through her life of extreme self-denial, through prayer and teaching, and through a steadfast fight for "the just order of the Church". Above all, though, it is Catherine's efforts in bringing Pope Gregory XI back from Avignon and her subsequent support for the ill-fated Urban VI that are highlighted. William sees the period of the Avignon papacy as comparable to the Babylonian captivity of Israel and laments the fact that the Church paid little attention to Catherine's reforming activities.

William does not dwell on the fact that the papal return to Rome was so short-lived, which could risk implying that Catherine's work was for nothing. Instead he suggests that her mission had been accomplished and hopes for better things in the future:

> The works and toils which she sustained for the Church provide
> a testimony for her, for the true faith that our Lord Urban VI is
> the true pope. Many were enlightened by her, and perhaps many
> will yet be enlightened: *In your light we shall see light* (Ps 36:10).

Typically, memorial sermons were peppered with scriptural quotations, especially from the Old Testament, and William's sermon is no exception. Towards the end he strikes an apocalyptic note, quoting Ezekiel 32:7, "I will cover the sun with a cloud, and the moon shall not give its light." He comments:

---

[42]   See generally, D. L. D'Avray, *Death and the Prince: Memorial Preaching before 1350* (Oxford: Oxford University Press, 1994).

> I take the sun to mean the Catholic Church of God, militant under our Lord Pope Urban VI, which shines with the power and light of the Catholic faith . . . At the hour of her death, as I have heard, [Catherine] said to her sons: "For the sake of this faith, that is, that our Lord Urban VI is the true pope, you should if necessary expose yourselves to death." Indeed, even in this present life she was clothed with the sun that is, she burned with a zealous desire for the reformation of the Church.[43]

There is much else that could be said about this remarkable document, which several times digresses into an invective against the "men of Siena" who failed to recognize Catherine's sanctity, and which presents her suffering in messianic terms, alluding to verses from Isaiah 53: "It was as if the Lord put all our iniquities onto her. She was sacrificed for the Church of God because it was her own will, and she did not open her mouth."

But what remains particularly significant is how the sermon format is used above all to commemorate one particular episode in Catherine's life, to commend this to those who come after her, and to portray her as fully committed to the service of the Church. Although William refers a number of times to her mystical experiences and to her extreme fasting practices, he places these too in the context of her longing for reform. Describing her life as "not only a martyrdom but many martyrdoms, both in flesh and in the spirit", William argues that the martyrdoms of the spirit were the greater, "especially when she saw that offenses against God abounded in the Church of God, when she saw the pastors of the Church in disarray".[44] Similarly, referring to Catherine's frequent mystical experiences on receiving Holy Communion, William describes her as suffering in rapture *for the Church of God* and for the Christian people", with severe consequences for her physical health.

Every biographical detail is therefore employed to illustrate Catherine's devotion to the Church and to the ending of the Avignon papacy. That is how we are to remember her.

---

[43] "Remembering Catherine", n. 41 above, p. 208.

[44] Ibid., p. 206.

Conclusion

The death of Catherine of Siena in 1380 marked the end of the unique group of holy women clustered in the Tuscany region. With the spread of literacy and ever greater ease of communications, a new phase in the history of holy women was rapidly developing elsewhere; yet the influence of the Tuscan women continued to be felt, as writers, artists and civic leaders built up their legacy.

Later holy women

The late fourteenth century saw the emergence of arguably the greatest name in English female mysticism, Julian of Norwich. Born in 1342, Julian was a near contemporary of Catherine of Siena, and remains best known for her *Revelations of Divine Love*, written around the end of the century. Thanks largely to her enclosed existence, very little is known about Julian's life beyond what is revealed in her writing, and still less about the source of her ideas. McGinn comments, "The breadth and depth of Julian's theology make it difficult to believe that she did not have access to a range of theological and spiritual authors, but it is impossible to determine how this material reached her."[1]

However, Julian's writings are firmly rooted in the Bible, and it would be surprising if there were no similarities with continental mystics who shared the same starting point. Yet McGinn's conclusion is that, unlike Catherine of Siena,

> [Julian] minimized, even broke with, many of the common teachings of late medieval theology and mysticism . . . Julian's mystical theology was, and probably is, too original, even too

---

[1]   Bernard McGinn, *The Varieties of Vernacular Mysticism (1350–1550)* (New York: Crossroad Publishing Co., 2012), p. 429.

radical, to receive any official status. She is radical, however, in
the truest sense of a thinker who has penetrated to the roots of the
mystery of love and who is therefore still very much present both
as a resource for contemporary theology and as an inspiration for
all who are seeking God.[2]

Born some thirty years after Julian and in a similar part of the world (the
East Anglian town of Lynn), Margery Kempe (1373–1440) was a very
different character. She shared with some of the Italian mystics a desire
to be free of her commitments to married life, a propensity for ecstatic
utterances, tears and fainting, and an enthusiasm for pilgrimage—to
Jerusalem and Rome in 1413–15 and to Compostela in or around 1417.
Margery's *Book* is autobiographical and is characterized by lengthy
conversations with God. Margery visited Syon Abbey, home to Brigittine
nuns, and would no doubt have been familiar with the English translation
of Bridget's *Revelations*. When she was in Rome in 1415, Margery visited
Bridget's house and met people who knew her, including Bridget's former
maidservant who told her that she was "kind and meek with everybody,
and that she had a laughing face", and an unnamed "good man" who
"little thought that she had been as holy woman as she was, because she
was always homely and kind with everybody who wanted to talk to her".[3]

Within Italy the fifteenth century saw the activities of two holy
women in the northern part of the peninsula, the Franciscan Catherine
of Bologna (1413–?62) and Catherine of Genoa (1447–1510), and to the
south, Rita of Cascia (d. 1456). Rita was a stigmatic, and her hometown,
north-east of Rome, is now a place of pilgrimage.

Catherine of Bologna has, unusually, a reputation as an artist, although
it is unclear how well founded that is. She is chiefly remembered for
her treatise, *Le sette armi spirituali* ("The seven spiritual weapons")
which is the first major work to survive that was written in a saint's
own hand. McGinn argues that her writings draw on both Angela of
Foligno and Catherine of Siena, and that she had an important role in

---

[2]   Ibid., p. 470.

[3]   B. A. Windeatt (tr. and ed.), *The Book of Margery Kempe* (Harmondsworth:
      Penguin Books, 1985), p. 132.

the dissemination of late medieval mysticism. Like Clare of Montefalco, obedience was central to her thinking, but less as a matter of loyalty to the Church than as "a way of attaining a profound sense of divine presence through self-annihilation".[4]

Catherine of Genoa is perhaps the best known of this later wave of Italian mystics, and the one most different from her predecessors. Catherine was a married noblewoman who came late to the religious life, following the death of her husband in 1497, although they had both devoted themselves to charitable works over more than twenty years and had renounced marital relations, having become Franciscan tertiaries. She is remembered particularly for her *Treatise on Purgatory* (*Trattato del Purgatorio di Santa Caterina da Genova)*, a text which bears the heading: "How by comparing it to the Divine Fire which she felt in herself, this soul understood what purgatory was like and how the souls there were tormented".[5] This short work examines the joy and love for God of the souls in Purgatory, a place where even in the suffering of being cleansed from sin, "the souls . . . enjoy the greatest happiness and endure the greatest pain; the one does not hinder the other."[6]

Conceptualization and re-conceptualization

By the close of the Middle Ages, Italy was altogether a more comfortable place to be a mystic than it had been a couple of centuries earlier. Third Orders, and the acceptance of women to them, were firmly established, and holy women were much more readily accepted by the Church. The association with civic life that was so marked in the lives of Margaret of Cortona and Catherine of Siena is continued in the stories of Catherine of Bologna and Catherine of Genoa.

As we have seen, the reputations of the Tuscan holy women were made and enhanced by their biographers and artists. This also works in reverse: the artist himself gains prestige from his subject, particularly when he

---

[4]   N. 1 above, p. 297.

[5]   Translation by Charlotte Balfour and Helen Douglas Irvine (1946) reproduced in Ray C. Petry (ed.), *Late Medieval Mysticism* (London: The Westminster Press, 1957), pp. 399–413.

[6]   Ibid., p. 408.

is working in a notable civic context. Giorgio Vasari, in his *Lives of the Artists* (compiled over a period from 1549 to 1568), includes the life of the Sienese painter Domenico Beccafumi (1486–1551). Vasari describes in some detail Domenico's panel painting in S. Benedetto, "the property of the monks of Monte Oliveto outside the Tufi gate", depicting Catherine of Siena receiving the stigmata and other episodes in Catherine's life, which, he comments, "for its extremely soft colouring and its great relief was and is still highly praised".[7] Another panel, this time in the church of Santo Spirito, which includes Catherine of Siena's mystical marriage, is said to have "won great honour for Domenico, as did a number of small figures painted on the predella of the panel which show . . . Christ presenting to Saint Catherine of Siena two crowns, one of roses and another of thorns, and Saint Bernardino of Siena preaching to an enormous crowd in the main square of Siena".[8]

Just as Catherine of Siena's reputation was enhanced by an association with Katherine of Alexandria, so artists could in turn bolster the reputation of later saints, such as Rita of Cascia, by setting them alongside the Sienese saint. Similarly, artists could imitate previous depictions of mystical marriage or stigmatization, to align their more recent subjects with saints of the past. An example of this is in Faenza Cathedral, where a shaft of light links the forehead of the crucified Christ with the forehead of Rita of Cascia, leaving a wound caused by the crown of thorns, a replica of which Rita is holding in front of her.

The formulaic nature of the medieval *Legenda* ensured the decline of the genre. In more recent times, however, their purpose lives on in works of popular piety. Mauriac's use of the story of Margaret Cortona is unusual in that it is written by an established literary figure. By contrast, there is a large amount of twentieth-century popular fiction, of varying quality, devoted to Catherine of Siena, thanks, no doubt, to the longer biographical form chosen by Raymond of Capua having provided a wealth of material for novelists to work with.

Diarmaid MacCulloch writes of medieval mystics:

---

[7]   Julia Conaway Bondanella and Peter Bondanella (tr.), Giorgio Vasari, *The Lives of the Artists* (Oxford: Oxford University Press, 1991), p. 379.

[8]   Ibid., p. 380.

> The mystic met God beyond the mediation of the male Church hierarchy, and in ways which can be remarkable metaphorical or imaginative appropriations of physical contact with the divine. Characteristic in mystical writings of the period are expressions which emphasize the human vulnerability, frailty, virginity of the subject, but which also celebrate the capacity of this frailty to unite with the divine.[9]

For the holy women whose spirituality set them apart from the Church in their day, it is perhaps this vulnerability that has enabled subsequent generations of writers and artists, and indeed the Church itself, to portray them in terms that best suit their different agendas. As the example of the Italian holy women shows, this has not been dishonouring to them. Rather, it has set them in a tradition of their own which has preserved their memory and established a recognizable pattern that transcends the cultural specifics of their time. Already by the fifteenth century, for lay people in the Christian West, this had resulted in their religion being set free to "retreat out of the sphere of public ritual into the world of the mind and the imagination".[10]

---

[9] Diarmaid MacCulloch, *A History of Christianity* (London: Allen Lane, 2009), p. 421.

[10] Ibid., p. 566.

Index

CPSIA information can be obtained
at www.ICGtesting.com
Printed in the USA
BVHW061322270122
627358BV00009B/449